101 SECRETS of CANADIAN CULTURE

by Catherine (Kate) Maven

First Printing: 2019

ISBN: 978-1-9992486-6-6

NOTE: The material contained in this book is set out in good faith for general guidance and no liability can be accepted for loss or expense incurred as a result of relying in particular circumstances on statements made in the book. The laws and regulations of Canada are complex and liable to change, and readers should check the current situation with the relevant authorities before making personal arrangements.

Otter-Girl Press
Burlington, Ontario, Canada

https://sleepingcat.wixsite.com/ottergirlpress

With love and gratitude
to all of my ESL students
who inspired me
to write this book.

You make me
PROUD
to be a
CANADIAN!

Other Books by Catherine Maven

- **101 Secrets of Canadian Culture** – Teacher's Workbook
- **How I Live With Wanting to Die** (My Journey Toward Healing)
- **Bedtime Mindfulness** (Questions for Parents & Kids)
- **Small Boobs & Gams** (satire of extreme makeovers)

For Children:

- **Alien Animals Stole Our Alphabet** (rhyming - handwriting & alphabet book)
- **Alien Animals Coloring Book**
- **How to Train Your Puppy:** A READ-it-YOURSELF Guide for KIDS
- **The Cat in King Arthur's Cloak** (picture book)
- **'Magination Molly** (picture book)
- **Splash Toes Creek** (illustrator & publisher)

Novels:

- **Coyote Summer** (YA fantasy novel)
- **Ex-Betty** (science-fiction novel, quarter-finalist for Amazon Breakthrough Authors competition)

Table of Contents

INTRODUCTION

Many of the social rules in Canada aren't clearly explained anywhere, and newcomers and their families need to know these "secrets" if they want to succeed socially, as well as in schools, the workplace, and business. With a lifetime of experience in Canada as an ESL educator, a mother of three, and as a worker in banking, computers, marketing and employment counselling, I have discovered that we have a lot of unwritten rules. I have shared most of these secrets with my newcomer ESL students, who have told me that this information really helped them to integrate into Canada, and it is at their request that I wrote this book.

Keep in mind, however, that these are MY OPINIONS about things you should know. Since people come here from all over the world, there really is NO such thing as "Canadian Culture"! Canadians are NOT all the same – so I'm sure there will be Canadians who will disagree with some of my Secrets. That's okay, too. Part of the reason people come to Canada is for individual freedoms – including the freedom to disagree. So to those Canadians whose experiences are different from mine, I offer my apologies, and hope you will share your understanding of Canadian culture with the newcomers in your area. Volunteering with newcomers is a rewarding experience!

The first secrets are the obvious parts of Canadian Culture – the parts you probably read about before deciding to move here.

Then I move on to secrets that contain some ideas that may be familiar and some that may be new to you. Some of the secrets in this book are about our attitudes and laws regarding sexual relationships. I realize that you may come from a culture that has strong taboos against talking about sex, or where sexual relationships are much more closely controlled than is the case in many parts of Canada. Talking about sex is often taboo here, too, but one of the reasons that I wrote this book was to tell you things that you might not learn from ANYONE else!

So please forgive me if you find some of these secrets offensive. I'm NOT suggesting that you or your children have to behave – or believe! – like we do. I just want you to UNDERSTAND a bit about why WE act the way we do, and what's (mostly) considered NORMAL in Canadian culture.

Finally, I share secrets about the DARK parts of Canadian Culture – the prejudices that we try very hard to pretend that we don't have. (But, of course, we do have because we're human beings just like everyone else in the world. I'm optimistic enough to believe that MOST Canadians practice tolerance, but realistic enough to understand that prejudices exist here, too.)

I've included some topics to Google, too, if you want further information about some of the topics in this book.

Okay. Here are the **101 most important secrets** I've learned for succeeding socially, as well as in Canadian schools and workplaces. I have placed a simple-English version of each secret on the front of the page, and a more detailed explanation on the back, because I'm trying to make this book useful to newcomers with a wide range of English comprehension.

Secret #1:

Expect

CULTURE SHOCK

You will ALWAYS need to learn more about the cultures & customs of your neighbours & coworkers.

SECRET #1: MULTICULTURALISM

You probably already KNOW that Canada is a multicultural society. But that is also why it's almost IMPOSSIBLE to write a book about "Canadian Culture". My ESL students ask me, "What's Canadian food?" and I tell them, "Well, I grew up eating British, French, Italian, Mexican, ~~Russian~~ and Chinese food." LOL!

If more than 20% of Canadians weren't born here, of COURSE you're going to be interacting with people from amazingly different races, creeds and cultures. Especially if you come from a monoculture (a place where almost everyone is the same race, religion & culture), you're probably going to be experiencing CULTURE SHOCK over and over again. (I know *I* STILL am!)

The most important thing to remember is to SHOW RESPECT & TOLERANCE toward EVERYONE (and expect them to show it to YOU). It's normal to feel strange, and even a bit afraid, of people who seem to be acting SO differently from the way you were raised. It's sometimes hard to understand WHY people act the way they do! Please be PATIENT - with them - and with YOURSELF. It takes time to adapt. It takes time to feel like Canada is your HOME, too.

- And CELEBRATE the differences! It's okay to ask questions about clothing, food or practices that you don't understand, as long as you are RESPECTFUL. Learn about your neighbours & coworkers. It will enrich your life!

Secret #2:
Yep. We really ARE that Polite

We usually say "Please",
"Thanks" & "You're Welcome"
to EVERYONE.
We Say
"Sure" rather than "Yes"
and
"Sorry" rather than "No".

SECRET #2: COURTESY

I'm sure you hear us say Please, Thanks, You're Welcome and Sorry ALL the time. You might wonder WHY. Well, firstly, our culture (in Ontario at least) is mostly handed down from British culture, which is SUPER polite.

Secondly, since we are often dealing with people who are VERY different than us, we need to be CAREFUL not to offend. If I don't know what's okay and not okay to you, I'm EXTRA-Polite, just to be on the safe side.

We don't usually say, "Yes", we say "SURE!" We don't usually say "No", we say "SORRY." When someone asks you a "Yes/No" question, it's NOT polite to give a one-word answer! That's why you'll hear us say, "Yes, I do" or "No, I don't".

We also DON'T usually say, "I don't like _____". If someone asks us if we like something – but we DON'T like it, we say, "I don't really care for _____" (food or drink) or "I'm not really interested in _____" (activities or conversation topics).

If someone OFFERS us food or drink – such as, "Would you like some coffee?" the polite response is "Yes, please" or "No, thanks".

NOTE: if a Canadian offers you a drink when you arrive at their house, **ALWAYS** say "**Yes, please**" because they MAY NOT OFFER AGAIN!!

Secret #3: SMILE!!

Canadians smile at our neighbours, friends & everyone at work, whether we know them or not. In big cities, though, we usually DON'T smile at strangers on the street.

SECRET #3: SMILE!!

You have probably noticed how COMMON it is for Canadians to smile. You might think that Canada is like Disney World – "The Happiest Place on Earth"! Of course, that's not entirely true. While Canada is currently the 13th happiest country in the world (in 2023), we're not ALL happy, ALL the time.

But it's an important part of our culture to FOCUS on the POSITIVE. When Canadian employers are asked, "What is the most important quality you look for in a new employee?" one of the Top 10 Soft Skills is "Friendliness". We don't usually smile in court, but we SHOULD smile (and make lots of EYE CONTACT!) during MOST job interviews.

In big cities, we don't smile at strangers on the streets, but in smaller towns, it's normal for complete strangers to smile at you and say, "Good morning!"

We smile at the cashier in the grocery store, at the bank teller, and even at the police officer who stops us for speeding.

Smiling "breaks the ice" and makes people more likely to become your friend.

By now, you're probably wondering, "Do people smile at me when they're angry at me?" Not always, but it IS kind of hard to tell if someone REALLY likes you or is just smiling to be polite. Actually, when people feel comfortable enough to be your friend, they may actually smile LESS!

Secret #4:

WHY ARE WE SO PEACEFUL?

Because Canadians practice TOLERANCE & RESPECT for *EVERYONE.*

SECRET #4: TOLERANCE & RESPECT

Related to our value of being POLITE, Canadians are, in general, very TOLERANT and RESPECTFUL of everyone, even when they seem quite STRANGE to us!

Because we come from all over the world, there is really NO SUCH THING as "CANADIAN CULTURE"! Every group, every family, and even every INDIVIDUAL may hold very different VALUES and ETHICS. What I'm trying to do in this book is reveal some GENERAL rules and SECRET rules that apply to MANY Canadians – but certainly not ALL.

The ONE thing that DOES unite us, I think, is that regardless of how DIFFERENT you are from us, we respect your RIGHT to believe what you believe and to ACT in a way that makes sense to you (as long as you're not BREAKING the LAW).

I think TOLERANCE is one of our HIGHEST values. We might criticize others in the privacy of our own homes, but when we're dealing with each other in public, we keep our opinions to ourselves.

Some of my immigrant students call this "hypocrisy", but it's part of what makes Canada a PEACEFUL country.

Secret #5:
Gender Identity

You should treat EVERYONE in Canada with respect & tolerance.

You are FREE to believe whatever you want, but we *respect* people's sexual orientation the same way we do their religion or culture.

SECRET #5: GENDER IDENTITY

Being gay is still illegal in many countries, and frowned upon in many others. However, our Charter of Rights & Freedoms GUARANTEES our rights, and that includes sexual orientation.

In Canada, being "straight" or LGBTQ+ is all considered NORMAL. If you have a son or daughter who is gay, you might want to read: Always My Child: A Parent's Guide to Understanding Your Gay, Lesbian, Bisexual, Transgendered, or Questioning Son or Daughter

Straight = a man in a relationship with a woman or vice-versa.

L = Lesbian (2 women)

G = Gay (2 men)

B = Bisexual (liking partners of both sexes)

T = Transsexual (born in the body of one gender, but identifying with the opposite gender – or NO gender!)

Q = Queer or Questioning (not sure of one's sexual orientation, or REFUSING to be identified in a single way)

I can't force you to accept that this is normal, but as I tell my ESL students, "You came here for peace and safety. Well, one of the reasons that Canadians are so peaceful is that we practice TOLERANCE of those who are DIFFERENT than we are."

Secret #6:

GREETINGS:

DON'T Say "Hello" or "Goodbye"

Canadians are Polite, but

INFORMAL.

Say, "Hi!"

and

"See you!"

SECRET #6: "Hello" and "Goodbye"

It's not WRONG to say these things – they're just very FORMAL to us, so you don't sound that FRIENDLY when you speak this way.

Friends say, "Hi" or "Good morning!" when they see each other, and "See you! Bye!" when we're leaving.

Other Ways to say Hello:

- What's up?
- How's it going?
- Hiya!
- Sup! (short for 'What's up?') – usually young men

When you haven't seen someone in a long time:

- Nice to see you!
- Nice to see you again!
- I haven't seen you in forever!
- Long time no see!
- What's new?
- What have you been up to?

Other Goodbyes:

- See you _____ (tomorrow, Monday, etc.)
- Great seeing you!
- Take care
- Sorry, gotta go.
- Have a good _____ (day, weekend). *
- Bye-bye!
- Take it easy

* *NOTE:* "Have a good one!" is used by CSRs (customer service representatives) but NOT with friends and family.

Secret #7:

Only ask, "How are you?" once in awhile

We usually ONLY shake hands the FIRST time we meet, and DON'T ask "How are you?" every day.

SECRET #7: GREETINGS

In many countries, it's customary to shake hands with your coworkers and boss every day, and to ask everyone, "How are you?" every time you see them.

In Canada, though, we normally only shake hands the FIRST time we meet, or if we haven't seen that person in a long time. Some young people don't even shake hands the first time. They just raise a hand and say, "Hey" when they meet you.

We usually only ask, "How are you?" if we haven't seen someone in a while. The answer is, "Good, thanks, and you?" (We only say "Fine" to STRANGERS!) On Mondays, we normally ask, "How was your weekend?" instead of "How are you?"

If you have started a new course or job, or else have been sick or injured, we ask, "How are you doing?" – or if it's your child, "How is he/she doing?"

Close friends and family may HUG every time they see each other – and we often hug our kids every day when they come home from school. Women are more likely to hug women, and men may or may not hug men. Hugging between men and women – unless it's family or a close friend – is not that common. We may also hug for goodbye.

Secret #8:
Learn SMALL TALK

We "break the ice" at the beginning of a conversation by talking about the weather, sports, kids, or pets.

SECRET #8: SMALL TALK

Maybe you're wondering just WHY everyone is always talking about the stupid WEATHER!! Well, there are 2 reasons: the first one is, if you live in Phoenix, Arizona (which gets 299 days of sunshine a year!), people DON'T usually talk about the weather. But in many parts of Canada, we have a joke: "If you don't like the weather, wait 3 hours. It's SURE to CHANGE!"

The second reason is that the weather is a "safe" topic. Nobody is going to be offended if you start talking about the weather. We guard our privacy quite seriously, so if you start a conversation by asking the price of my sweater or how well my kids did on their report cards, I'm going to think you are NOSY and may not want to be your friend!

We don't usually start conversations with close friends and family with talk about the weather. We can get personal with them almost immediately, asking about their health, spouse, kids, car, home or pets. I know it's WEIRD for many immigrants to talk about pets, but pets are FAMILY to us. (See Secret # 89)

With VERY close friends and family, we can also discuss TABOO subjects such as politics, religion, money, sexuality, and so on.

With strangers, acquaintances, neighbours or coworkers, though, we're careful to steer conversations away from "taboo" subjects (see **Secret #9**).

Secret #9:
TABOO Subjects

We <u>don't</u> usually talk to strangers or acquaintances about:

Age

Money

Religion

Politics

Sexuality or Sex

SECRET #9: TABOO SUBJECTS

This is another area where Canadians may be VERY different from people in your home country. In Korea, for example, you basically MUST tell your age immediately, because you should speak to the "older" person using terms of respect.

In Canada, though, it's quite RUDE to ask anyone's age, and we don't normally TELL our age except to friends. We also don't ask or tell ANYTHING about money because as long as we don't know how much money you have in comparison to ourselves, we can Pretend we are EQUALS (see **Secret #93**).

We also avoid talking about sexuality, religion or politics. These are subjects that people often feel very strongly about – and may not AGREE about – and Canadians HATE conflict!! In many other countries, you can ENJOY a heated argument about the government or a religion, but unless you are VERY close friends, we aren't likely to risk having an argument with you.

If you REALLY want to ask a personal question, you need to ASK PERMISSION to ask. Use this structure: "Can I ask you your age?" or "Would you mind telling me how much you paid for your house?" This gives the other person the option of politely refusing to answer: "I'd rather not say."

Secret #10:

Don't ask Questions that are TOO PERSONAL

It's normal to ask people about their jobs and their kids, but we avoid asking "WHY?"

SECRET #10: TOUCHY SUBJECTS

Even once we get to know you, there are still subjects we don't like to talk about. "Why?" is generally a RUDE question here. If I leave my job, you probably want to know why, but you should ask, "Oh, what happened?" because it implies that there is a logical reason for the decision rather than an emotional one.

People here normally don't compare their kids' report card results. It's rude to ask, "How is _____ doing in Grade One?" because we think you're worried about her success. It's better to ask, "How does _____ like her new teacher and her class?" We might brag when our child wins an award, but then we expect YOU to brag about YOUR child, too!

If your son or daughter just started a new job, it's normal to ask, "How's he/she doing?"

We also don't ask "Why?" when someone tells us they've separated from their spouse or are getting a divorce. If you're a close friend, they'll volunteer the information, but we shouldn't ask.

If someone is having a health problem, we tread very carefully in asking about it, particularly if it's serious, like cancer. Some people are happy to talk about their health, and some people aren't.

Secret #11:

93% of

Communication is through TONE & BODY LANGUAGE

You need to learn how to use tone & body language to seem FRIENDLY.

SECRET #11: TONE & BODY LANGUAGE

Tone in English is used to convey emotions and intent. For speakers of languages where tone conveys part of the meaning of the word (e.g., Mandarin), this can be difficult to adapt to. A FRIENDLY tone has up-and-down inflections!

Practice saying, "***Really***" with the following tones:

TONE:	MEANING:
Low	Sad, depressed or angry
Flat (no inflection)	Bored, sad, *disbelief*
Rising	Question or disbelief
High, rising	Excitement or friendliness
Up then down	Emphasis
TOO Loud	THREATENING, maybe CRAZY

BODY LANGUAGE YOU SHOULD BE AWARE OF:

- Making eye contact means you are telling the truth.

- Crossed arms in front of your chest = hostile.

- Touching a person while you talk = romantic interest

- When you say, "Sorry", you should shrug (with 1 or both shoulders) and open hands in front of your body to show sincerity

- Tapping fingers or feet = impatience (and it's RUDE)

- Pointing with your index finger = RUDE! To point, use your whole arm, palm out, facing up

Secret #12:

RESPECT our Personal Space

Canadians expect you to stand a MINIMUM of ONE ARM'S LENGTH away from them.

SECRET #12: PERSONAL SPACE

In many countries, it's normal and even GOOD to stand very close to the person you're speaking to. My student from Poland told me that when 2 women are speaking, they often put their arm around the other person's waist. I told her that we only stand like that with a romantic partner.

The arms-length distance applies 360° around a person. In a lineup at the bank, you shouldn't stand any closer to my back than an arm's length.

Of course, in a crowded elevator or bus, this distance isn't possible, but most Canadians will be very uncomfortable during that time. If you were having a conversation before you got on a crowded elevator, the Canadian might wait until you get off before continuing the conversation!

On the bus, you might have noticed that Canadians sit as far away from each other as possible – which is, again, quite different from many other cultures. People may read or look at a device to avoid conversation with other riders!

This rule is especially important between men and women who don't know each other very well, and even MORE so when the man is a lot BIGGER than the woman. I feel threatened when a large man stands too close to me!

Secret #13:
AVOID Body Noises

If you sneeze, say, "Excuse me." The other person says, "Bless you!"
If you cough, cough into your elbow. AVOID making other body noises in front of other people.

SECRET #13: EMBARRASSING BODY NOISES

Let's be honest. Everyone farts from time to time! But Canadians prefer to leave the room (go into the bathroom if possible) to do this.

Sometimes, our stomach rumbles when we're hungry. There isn't much anyone can do to stop this, but having something to eat before you meet up with people can prevent it.

Other body noises – for example, clearing your throat or your sinuses, or chewing with your mouth open, are not socially acceptable, and should not be done in front of other people.

Related to this, SPITTING in public is RUDE!

If you have to blow your nose, sneeze, or cough, please turn away from other people. Sneeze into a tissue if possible. Cough into your elbow.

If you have a cold or the flu, please STAY HOME! We don't appreciate you sharing your virus with us!

Secret #14:
Public Displays of Emotion

Canadians accept seeing people HUG each other in public, but we don't usually KISS (or CRY) in front of others.

SECRET #14: Public Displays of Emotion

You might come from a country with VERY different social rules about showing emotions in public. In some cultures, for example, shouting or crying in public is normal and considered healthy.

Probably due to our British heritage, our culture promotes a "stiff upper lip" (meaning keep your emotions to yourself!) – and this is what makes us feel embarrassed when other people show strong emotions in public. We DON'T usually YELL or CRY in public.

Another unwritten rule at work is, "Leave your problems at the door." This means my personal issues shouldn't affect my ability to do my job or interact with the public. A Canadian might SMILE and act NORMAL a day or two after a loved one has died! It's NOT that we aren't as SAD as you would be; it's just that we feel we have to HIDE it.

SHOWING AFFECTION: Hugging in public has become more socially acceptable, but many Canadians still feel uncomfortable seeing a couple KISS in public.

Holding hands is (mostly) okay, though! Parents and children, men and women, old people – no problem! In some countries, it's normal for 2 women – or 2 men friends to hold hands in public, but many Canadians will assume they're in a romantic relationship!

Secret #15:

We are POLITE to Servers in Restaurants

We say, "Please" and "Thanks" & we DON'T snap our fingers to get their attention.

SECRET #15: RESTAURANT ETIQUETTE

You might be surprised to hear Canadians say, "Please" and "Thank you" to a server or bartender in a restaurant, but it's normal here. It's related to our value of EQUALITY – we respect that the server is doing his/her job, just as we do ours, so we give them the same respect that we want for ourselves.

To get your server's attention if you need them, first just try to make eye contact. DON'T snap your fingers or WAVE at them! If they don't see you or respond to you, you can lift your hand up beside your shoulder (not above) to signal for them to come over. Finally, if they STILL don't see you, it's okay to ask another server to get yours.

If you have a complaint about your meal, get the server's attention, and then tell them what the problem is. They should apologize and take your meal back to the kitchen. Often they will let you choose a different dish and you won't be charged for either! (This isn't a LAW, though, so they don't have to do so.)

Even in a fast-food restaurant, if there is a problem with your food or drink, you can take it back to the counter and they will usually replace the item for free.

Secret #16:
Who PAYS at the Restaurant?

Regardless of who invited, each person or couple usually pays their OWN bill. BEFORE ORDERING, We tell the server, "Separate checks."

SECRET #16: CANADIANS ARE CHEAPSKATES

I know I'm going to make some Canadians ANGRY by telling you this. But after learning how GENEROUS people are in other countries, I've come to think that we ARE kind of CHEAP.

In most countries, if I invite you to a restaurant, *I* should pay. If it's my birthday, I should invite my friends and *I* should pay. NOT TRUE in Canada!

Normally, each person (or couple) pays for their own food and drink. Before we order, we tell the server, "Separate checks". If I'm with my husband, we say, "One check for us two."

If it's my birthday and I go out with friends, though, each person will usually pay for their own food & drink, but the group will split MY check so that I don't have to pay ANYTHING.

Of course, there ARE exceptions. When a family goes out (regardless of the age of the kids, who might be adults), often the FATHER will pay for everyone. We used to call my dad "Mr. Wallet"! Close friends & family make also take turns paying (see **Secret #27**).

On a date, the man will often pay for the woman – though this is changing. Today, couples make TAKE TURNS paying.

Secret #17:

How MUCH should you TIP?

- Servers (15-25%)

- Bartenders (15-25%)

- Coffee / Tea Shops (10-15%)

- Fast Food (10-15%)

- Food Delivery (15% or round up)

- Beauty and Barber Shops (15-20%)

- Taxis (Round up about $5) … This means, if your cost is $26.50, give him/her $30. If it's $29.50, give him/her $35)

SECRET #17: MORE ABOUT TIPPING

TIPPING IN A HOTEL OR AIRPORT:

- Doorman: $3 to $5 - maybe more if he hails a taxi for you in the rain.

- Bellhop: $3 to $5 per bag delivered to your room

- Housekeeper: $2 to $5 a day for chain hotels and B&Bs. For luxury resorts, where rooms require more upkeep, tip $5 to $20 a day

- Room Service: 15 to 20%

- Concierge: $5 to $50, depending on whether the service was minor (booking you a restaurant reservation) or major (scoring hard-to-get tickets)

- Valet: $5 to $10. Tip when you PICK UP the car, not when you drop it off.

- Room Delivery: $2 to $5 per delivery (extra towels etc.)

- Spa Staffers: 15 to 20% (Leave the tip with the receptionist)

- Airport Shuttle Driver: $10

- Airport Porters: $2-$5 for the first bag and $2 for each additional bag; over-sized bags: $5 per bag

- Wheelchair captains: at least $5. If the wheelchair captain takes you to the restroom or does EXTRA: up to $20

Secret #18:

YOU are responsible for initiating FRIENDSHIPS

Canadians are typically RESERVED around strangers. YOU should invite your neighbours or coworkers if you want to make friends (but not at the same time)!!

SECRET #18: IT'S UP TO YOU to make friends

This probably goes against everything in your culture. Usually it is the HOST person who has the responsibility for making the NEWCOMER feel welcome. And in smaller towns (and some neighbourhoods in larger cities), this is true here, too. When I first moved to a small town in Southern Ontario, most of my neighbours came over with food to welcome me. ☺

But in general, because Canadians are mostly quite PRIVATE & RESERVED, it's up to YOU to break the ice. Whether at work, at your children's school, or in your neighbourhood, it's YOUR job to initiate friendships.

Start by SMILING at the people around you, and greeting them in a friendly voice: "Good morning! Beautiful day!" (Even when the weather is TERRIBLE – this will get a laugh, and of course, laughing is a GREAT way to break the ice!)

After a few weeks of daily greetings, people should be warming up to you. Then you can invite them out (or over to your place) for a coffee or tea. (See **Secret #24**)

Canadians are reserved, but FRIENDLY once you get to know us!

Secret #19:
Your kids should learn to SKATE & SWIM

Socializing among Canadian kids is typically done with Skating in the winter & Swimming in the summer.

SECRET #19: SKATING & SWIMMING = A MUST

In case you hadn't noticed, Canada has a LOT of water! I started my kids in swimming lessons at 8 MONTHS old because I was terrified they would drown (They DIDN'T).

In addition to this obvious safety reason, there's a strong SOCIAL reason for your kids to learn to skate and swim. As I said, parties among Canadian kids tend to include skating in the winter and swimming in the summer. If your child can't do either of these, they may not be invited!!

Swimming is considered the HEALTHIEST form of exercise, because it's low-impact (doesn't put that much strain on your joints) and quite aerobic.

I also encourage ADULTS to take up these activities, if you don't already do them. Many of my immigrant ESL students say they stay inside all winter because, "It's too cold to do anything outside." I tell them, "If you're planning to stay in Canada, it's a good idea to EMBRACE winter by learning how to skate or ski (downhill or cross-country)."

Of course, tobogganing (called "sledding" in the U.S.) is also TONS of FUN and a great activity for parents and kids to do together in the winter!

Secret #20:

Men should learn about HOCKEY (and maybe GOLF). Women can, too – of COURSE!

Small talk among Canadian men is often about Hockey. Managers often socialize together by playing Golf.

SECRET #20: CANADA'S RELIGION = HOCKEY???

If you ask someone what they know about Canada, the FIRST answer might be "Hockey!" Hockey IS our national sport, and something almost EVERY boy (and MANY girls!) learn to play when they are kids. WARNING! If you watch professional hockey, you may see BLOOD. Professional hockey can be a VIOLENT sport. I don't watch hockey, I refused to let ANY of my 3 sons play hockey because of the very-common danger of concussion (Though children's hockey teams are working to improve this).

Nevertheless, especially for MEN, being able to talk – at least BASICALLY – about hockey is an excellent ice-breaker. Hockey is exciting to watch. It's very fast-paced and full of action. There are good websites & YouTubes explaining the basic rules of hockey. Of course, many WOMEN in Canada are ALSO crazy about hockey!

GOLF: Not only do upper-managers often socialize by playing golf together, but in BUSINESS, we have a saying: "Contracts are SIGNED on the 19th Hole." There are only 18 holes on a golf course, so the "19th Hole" is the clubhouse, where players go for a drink and a snack after the game.

If you don't know how to play golf, most courses have a Golf Pro who can give you some lessons, and you can rent golf clubs to try it out.

Secret #21:

Where to MEET new friends

I recommend https://www.meetup.com/ for finding LOCAL social groups that share your interests. — Or talk to the parents of your children's friends.

SECRET #21: FINDING NEW FRIENDS

You left behind most (or all) of your social network when you moved to Canada, so you have to start building a new one here.

Aside from meetup.com (a Wonderful resource, FREE to join, to find FACE-To-FACE clubs with a HUGE variety of interests), you should try talking to other parents also standing around waiting for their kids/grandkids after school. If you're at a playground, ask, "Which one is yours?" and say something POSITIVE about the child, then point out yours. That should start a conversation!

There are 3 kinds of strangers you can almost ALWAYS start a conversation with in public:

1.   **Parents with a BABY** (housebound; probably DYING for a conversation!). Say to him/her, "What a CUTE baby! How old is he or she?"

2.   **Seniors** – They are often LONELY and WELCOME a conversation. Say to him/her, "Beautiful day, isn't it?" or "Crazy weather, eh?"

3.   **People walking a DOG** – for some reason, people walking dogs tend to be more open to conversation with strangers. Say to him/her, "What a CUTE dog! What kind is he or she?"

Secret #22:
How to START a friendship

Take your TIME. We are often SLOW to make friends. Ask QUESTIONS about his/her life (but NOT too PERSONAL).

SECRET #22: GETTING STARTED WITH A FRIEND

CONVERSATION is like TENNIS: a good TIP about keeping a conversation going is to remember, whatever they ask you, answer, and then add, "And YOU?" or "How about YOU?"

Here are some questions to help you get started with a new friend (Remember; only ASK about things YOU want to talk about!):

- What do you like to do in your free time?
- Do you have any hobbies?
    - How long have you been doing them?
    - How did you get started?
- What kind of food / music / books / movies / TV shows do you like?
- What's the last movie you saw?
- Can you recommend a good TV show?
- Are there any books you would really recommend I read?
- Do you know any great YouTubes I should see?
- Are there any comedians you really like?
- What good restaurants do you know of around here?
- What's your favourite place to visit?
- Children (if you both have kids, talk about them)
- ** Travel: people in Canada may not have travelled extensively, so it's best to ask, "What places near here (or in Canada) do you recommend that I visit? (People LOVE to recommend places they love!)

Secret #23:

DON'T be a COMPLAINER

Canadians HATE complainers. We try to focus on the POSITIVE in our lives.

Remember, SMILE!!

SECRET #23: DON'T BE A COMPLAINER

In many cultures, it's NORMAL to COMPLAIN – about your job, your in-laws, your spouse, your kids, your home, etc. It provides a common ground with the person if they have the same complaint.

And of course, WE complain, TOO! (That's what Friends are FOR!!) But we DON'T complain ALL the time; we don't complain at work, or with people we don't know very well. If you're a complainer at work, you may never get a promotion! Canadian employers are looking for LEADERS – leaders who will INSPIRE the people around them to do their BEST work. And you should NEVER complain about your BOSS! (You never know who might "snitch" on you! – See **Secret #71**)

It's EASY to complain about the weather. But if all you ever say to your new neighbour is, "Isn't this weather AWFUL?" they aren't going to want to spend much time with you!

Canadians try to focus on the POSITIVE.

For more information on COMPLAINING EFFECTIVELY, though, see **Secret #91**.

Secret #24:

How to Invite a new FRIEND

Invite your new friend for coffee or tea at 2 pm on a Saturday or Sunday. Keep the first visit SHORT.

SECRET #24: THAT FIRST MEETING

Okay, you've broken the ice, SMILED, and are ready to INITIATE a new friendship. How do you GET STARTED?

Typically, if there is someone we've met that we like, we will invite him or her for a coffee or tea at 2 pm on a Saturday or Sunday. (NOT usually Lunch or Dinner!) If you know the person is FREE in the evenings, 7 pm is a good time, too.

You could invite them out to a coffee shop or to your home. A coffee shop might be best for the first time. You say, "Say, _____ (name), would you like to meet for a coffee?" They might answer, "How about a beer/wine?" – That's a Good sign! It means they feel comfortable enough around you to be honest about their preference.

We usually keep the first meeting short – probably about one to two hours. After an hour at a coffee shop, you might say, "Well, this has been great, but I really have to get going." If they like you, they might say, "Okay, but let's do this again soon!" (Yeah!!)

Men & Women: It's HARD to generalize about male/female friendships, because everyone is different, but if a man asks me out for coffee, I clarify that I'm married and it's NOT a date (but will add that some of my BEST friends are men!)

Secret #25:

Who can you SOCIALIZE with at Work?

We usually only socialize with people at our own level in the company. We DON'T invite our BOSS (but he/she CAN invite you).

SECRET #25: WHO CAN WE SOCIALIZE WITH?

Canadians value equality, but we tend to have fairly strict – and usually unwritten! – rules about who we can socialize with at work (and some companies actually have a POLICY about this). For example, a teacher shouldn't socialize with his/her ESL students.

You MIGHT socialize with clients – having a "business lunch" or a "Lunch and Learn" with a customer or client is quite common in sales or customer-service relationships.

We usually only socialize with our PEERS – my coworkers who I don't supervise. If I socialize with a subordinate, they feel PRESSURED to be NICE to me; it's considered inappropriate to put them in this position.

We also don't usually socialize with our BOSS, either. We certainly can't invite him/her out for a coffee! (But he/she can invite YOU.) We don't invite our boss (or our Teacher!) to a party at our house, a BBQ, or a wedding. It puts that person in an awkward position. If they say, "No", you might start to resent them.

Once the working relationship ends, however, you are FREE to develop a friendship. Two of my BEST friends used to be my bosses!!

Secret #26:

How to make FRIENDS at WORK

Every Friday, ask their plans for the weekend & remember to ask about those plans on Monday. Ask about their kids and pets. (Pets are also FAMILY here.)

SECRET #26: MAKING FRIENDS AT WORK

We are often slow to make friends at work. This might be hard to recognize, because Canadians tend to be very FRIENDLY, and you might think that that means they LIKE you! Unfortunately, it's not necessarily TRUE. We are usually friendly to EVERYONE (regardless of what we REALLY think of them).

You have to 'warm them up' by asking about their plans for the weekend, or what they did the previous evening. Just don't ask the same question EVERY day! LOL

In the morning, you might ask, "Did you do anything fun last night?" This gives them a chance to either share something fun that YOU might also enjoy, or to COMPLAIN about a problem they had. (I know, I SAID we don't complain, but I didn't mean NEVER …)

On Friday, ask, "Any plans for the weekend?" Pay attention to their answer, because you should follow up on Monday by asking how it went.

If the person was going out for dinner or to a movie, ask, "How was the meal/movie?" If they were hosting a get-together, ask, "How did your get-together go?" (That means, was it a success? Did you have any problems?)

Secret #27:
TAKE TURNS socially

We usually take turns Hosting. If you invited me last time, I should invite you this time.

SECRET #27: TAKING TURNS

Just like we expect children to take turns when playing games, we also take turns socially. This means if I (or my family and I) went to your house for dinner last month, this month I should invite you and your family to my place. It doesn't have to be exactly 50/50 (For example, if you have a swimming pool and I DON'T, my kids are going to be MUCH happier to go to YOUR place in the summer than your kids are to come to mine – but in that case, I should BRING FOOD when I come so that you aren't always cooking for us).

This also applies to 'play-dates' and sleepovers between children. If my child went to your house for a few hours, then *I* got a mini-vacation, so it's only FAIR to reciprocate so that YOU can have a mini-vacation, too! If I have 1 child and you have 2, but their ages are close, I should invite BOTH of your children for the play-date.

Carpooling, too. There might be 4-5 parents who share carpooling duties. So I will only be responsible for driving 4-5 kids to school once a week or so.

This also applies to "Who pays?" When my mother or my best friend and I go out for lunch, she pays one time and I pay the next time. (With family and very close friends, we don't usually do "separate checks".)

Secret #28:
How to RESPOND to an Invitation

YES: "Sure, thanks, I'd love to!"

NO: "Sorry, I can't this time. How about another time?"

MAYBE: "Sorry, I have to check. Can I let you know by Friday?" (Give a clear deadline.)

SECRET #28: RESPONDING TO INVITATIONS

GREAT! Someone's invited you to do something with them! So how do you respond?

If we're invited out for coffee – "Would you like to go grab a coffee tomorrow after work?" – the answer is simple:

"Sure! Thanks! I'd love to! Where and what time?"
– or, "Sorry, I'm tied up tomorrow. How about _____?" (e.g., <u>Friday</u> – or – Suggest an alternate day)
– or, "I'm not sure. I might have to work late. Can I let you know by _____ (lunchtime tomorrow?" – Give a <u>clear</u> deadline.

If you're invited over for a meal, you should say, "I'd love to, thanks! What can I bring?" Your host will probably answer, "Nothing. Just your lovely self / lovely family." But you should always bring SOMETHING! (See **Secret #31**)

Another way to say "No" is "Sorry, we have other plans for _____ (Saturday night). Can I have a rain-check?"

(A rain-check is a promise from a grocery store to honour a coupon price if they run out of the thing advertized. So asking for a rain-check means, "Please invite me for another time.")

Secret #29:
Can I BRING the KIDS?

MAYBE NOT. Unlike other cultures, unless we invite "You *and your family*", you shouldn't bring the kids.

SECRET #29: CAN I BRING THE KIDS?

If someone invites you to their place for a meal – "Would you like to come over for dinner on Saturday night?" – it's a bit complicated. In Canada, "you" means "JUST YOU". It DOESN'T mean your spouse or children are automatically invited. The person who invited you may not even KNOW you have a spouse and/or children!

You SHOULDN'T ask, "Can I bring my kids?" The best way to clear this up is to say something like, "Oh, thanks, I'd Love to, but I'll have to check with my husband/wife and see if he/she can take care of the kids." – or "I'd Love to, but I'll have to see if I can get a babysitter."

Both of those answers prompt the other person to clarify if you can bring your spouse and kids. Sometimes, they'll say, "Oh! Bring the whole family!" and sometimes they'll say, "Okay, can you find out and let me know?" (This means, it's an 'adult only' get-together and they'd prefer if you DIDN'T bring your children. This is NOT RUDE in Canada!)

Sometimes, we have 'Women Only' parties and the guys have 'Poker Night' or 'Hockey Night', where the women aren't invited. This is considered a normal part of our culture, so you'd better CHECK rather than show up with your kids!

Secret #30:
What TIME should you ARRIVE?

If you're invited for 6 pm, you should arrive about 6:10-6:20. Arriving an HOUR late is RUDE! (And don't EVER arrive EARLY!!)

SECRET #30: WHEN IS THE RIGHT TIME TO ARRIVE?

Canadians are usually quite punctual, and we expect other people to be, as well. Arriving 15-20 minutes late is absolutely okay, but arriving an HOUR late is RUDE. I realize that other cultures are much more relaxed about time than we are, but if I've prepared a meal that's ready at 6:30 pm and you show up at 7:30 pm, the meal may be RUINED!

It's also important NOT to come EARLY. I tell my ESL students that if I've invited friends to come at 6 pm, at 5:30 pm I may still be VACUUMING, and THEN I need a SHOWER!! If we're having a big party, I might ASK my CLOSEST family members or friends to come early to help me prepare, but unless we ask, DON'T COME EARLY!

If you invite us for 6 pm – you guessed it! We'll probably arrive about 6:10 – 6:15 pm, so DON'T EXPECT us to be LATE! One of my closest friends invited me to her (Pakistani) wedding, which started at 7 pm. When I arrived, there was NOBODY in the building!! I eventually found her in a small room with only her dad.

When I asked where her mom & bridesmaids were, she laughed. "They'll be here in about an hour," she said. "I asked you for 7 pm so we wouldn't be alone until they arrived!"

Secret #31:

What should you BRING?

When we're invited for dinner, we normally bring wine or dessert.

SECRET #31: WHAT TO BRING

There's often a LOT of culture shock in adjusting to Canadian culture. In many countries, if you invite me over and I bring food or drink, it's INSULTING! *(Did I think you wouldn't have food and drink available??)*

However, in Canadian culture, it's RUDE to come empty-handed (except with our CLOSEST friends and family members). It's normal for us to bring wine or a dessert. If I know you don't drink alcohol, I'll bring a dessert. If I know you like wine, I might bring a new wine for you to try.

If a Canadian invites you, it's wonderful if you bring a dessert from your home country. Most Canadians enjoy experiencing foods from different countries. We don't normally bring a main-dish, though, because it might not work with the meal that the host has planned.

If we're invited to a party or get-together with a number of other guests, it's usually BYOB (see **Secret #32**). This might also seem rude to you, but is normal to us!

Secret #32:
BYOB
(Bring Your Own Beverage)

Normally, when we're invited to a get-together, we bring whatever we'd like to drink (alcohol or non-alcoholic drinks).

SECRET #32: BYOB

This might be one of the biggest culture-shocks for you! As I said, if we're invited to a party or get-together with a number of other guests, it's usually **BYOB – Bring Your Own Beverage** (except tea or coffee – unless you want a very specific type).

I realize that if I brought my own beverage to your house in your country of birth, it would be INSULTING, but it's okay here.

When I was growing up, and my parents had a party, they would buy a LOT of alcohol, soft drinks, soda, and juice for their guests to drink. Since neither of my parents drank much beyond the occasional beer, a LOT of the 'booze' (slang for alcohol) would be left over, and sit for months or years in a cupboard – until the next party.

Over time, Canadians realized how wasteful this was, and people started bringing their own drinks. At first, it was BYOB – Bring Your Own Booze – and the host would provide other drinks. Then people got more particular about their drinks – Coke, Diet Coke, Coke Zero, etc. etc. – and we started to bring whatever we wanted to drink.

It's important to note that even if I only want 1 beer, I should bring a 6-pack. If I want 1 glass of wine, I should still bring a bottle. If I only want a glass or 2 of pop, I should still bring a 2 litre bottle. Bring enough to SHARE!

Secret #33:

A BBQ is DIFFERENT than a PARTY

If you're invited to a BBQ, it's CASUAL. Wear jeans or shorts and bring a salad or dessert & maybe a bottle of wine.

SECRET #33: BBQ, GET-TOGETHER, or PARTY?

If you are inviting people to your place for a meal in the evening, there's a DIFFERENCE between these 3 options:

BBQ: a barbeque is a VERY informal event. People will show up in shorts or jeans & t-shirts. If the weather is nice, the people will mostly stay outside in the back yard. The host may have speakers set up to play music outside. It's normally BYOB, plus we might also bring a salad or dessert and a bottle of wine as a gift for the host.

GET-TOGETHER: a get-together is another very informal event. It's when 2 families or a small group of friends meet at someone's house, a park or a restaurant to socialize. There is no special REASON for this event. If we go to someone's home, it's BYOB, plus we might also bring dessert and/or a bottle of wine as a gift for the host.

PARTY: a party is a special event, a celebration of some kind – like a birthday, anniversary, graduation, retirement, etc. Often there is a THEME, and you might be told a **dress code** (Google it!) Because these events are often held at a restaurant or are CATERED, guests usually only bring FLOWERS, a GIFT or a CARD for the person or people we are celebrating.

Secret #34:

When should you GO HOME?

We normally end social visits around midnight (unless you bring younger children; then 8-9 pm).

SECRET #34: WHEN TO GO HOME

I've learned from my ESL students that there is a BIG difference in 'time to go home' among different cultures! In some countries, you should stay VERY late and then are WELCOME to sleep over. In others, you should go home at 8 pm.

In Canada, we don't usually sleep over at anyone else's place – unless we've had a LOT to drink and they are close friends or family. Most people will head home around 11 pm to midnight if they don't have children, and around 8 to 9 pm if they have younger kids. (Of course, there are a LOT of differences between individuals, but this is a general guideline.)

Canadians are often pretty strict about their kids' bedtime, so don't be surprised if your guests rush out the door at 7 pm because it's 'baby's bedtime'!

If our guests don't appear to be leaving at the right time, we might stifle a yawn, or look at our watch to indicate it's getting late and you should GO. Then you should say, "Oh, look at the time! We really should be going!" – and your host will say, "Oh, do you have to?" – and you should say, "Sorry, yes, it's been LOVELY, thank you, but we have to get up early tomorrow."

Secret #35:
Are you MARRIED?

It's NOT a polite question. Many Canadian couples live "Common-Law" (not officially married, but living together).

SECRET #35: ARE ALL 'MARRIED' PEOPLE MARRIED?

Because some Canadians decide not to marry, or are divorced, it's NOT POLITE to ask "Are you married?" or "Do you have any kids?" (Ask "Do you have family here?")

About 15-20% of adult Canadians are living "Common-Law". This means that they are living together as IF they were married, but they have never gone through an official wedding ceremony and don't have a marriage licence. They might introduce their partner as "my partner", "my husband" or "my wife".

In many countries, this is considered a sin, but for us, there is no shame in living together without being officially married. Exactly what constitutes a "common-law" marriage varies from province to province, but in Ontario, if you've been living together for 1 year, you MUST file a joint tax return. Most companies will provide health benefits to a common-law spouse.

In the eyes of the government and for the purposes of taxes or custody of children, there is often NO difference between a common-law and a legal marriage, but it varies between provinces or territories, so check out the laws for your own region.

However, NOTE: most provinces and territories do NOT offer common-law partners the same RIGHTS to INHERITANCE or DIVISION OF PROPERTY as a married couple, so research that as well. You are not legally entitled to make financial or health decisions for a common-law spouse, either. **A Power of Attorney, Power of Attorney for Personal Care, and a Will** can provide these rights to a common-law spouse (in Ontario, at least).

Secret #36:

Men & Women - Equality

Men & Women in Canada try to treat each other as EQUALS. Decisions, Childcare, Finances & Housework are SHARED responsibilities.

SECRET #36: EQUALITY BETWEEN MEN & WOMEN

This is another topic where the DIFFERENCES between individual Canadians may be BIGGER than the SIMILARITIES. Every couple and every family has their own perceptions of the rights and roles of men and women.

For instance, for my mother and father, there were 'pink'jobs and 'blue' jobs around the house. My mother cooked, cleaned, did laundry & shopping and took care of the kids ('pink' jobs). My father took care of the car, mowed the grass, took out the garbage, shovelled the snow, and fixed stuff around the house ('blue' jobs). My mother considers herself a feminist, but was happy with this division of labour.

Today, women and men usually SHARE responsibility for finances, childcare, housework and decision-making. Even if they earn a lot less (see **Secrets 81 & 95**), women often contribute their share to the costs of running a home, and even if they work full-time, men often contribute to child-rearing, housework and cooking.

SADLY, even if both men and women work full-time, wives STILL do 50% more housework than husbands in Canada.

Secret #37:

CHILDREN are TREASURED but INDEPENDENT

Canadian kids usually have more FREEDOM but also more RESPONSIBILITIES.

SECRET #37: CANADIAN KIDS

It can be difficult to adjust to PARENTING in Canada. What you see, and what your KIDS see, is that most Canadian kids seem to have a lot more FREEDOM than kids do in your home country. Canadian kids seem to be more INDEPENDENT and LESS RESPECTFUL of parents or authority.

You're not entirely wrong! Just as we try to treat all adults with respect, we also try to show respect to our kids. From the outside, that looks like leniency. Our kids seem to be running the show!

But what you usually CAN'T see is that many of our kids usually ALSO have a lot more RESPONSIBILITY than your kids do. They probably have CHORES to do from about the age of 6, and may start helping with the cooking and laundry at about age 12. Many 15 year olds in Canada have part-time jobs (up to 30 hours a WEEK).

We treasure our kids, but we TRAIN them to be INDEPENDENT adults. By the time they start college or university, most of them (BOYS and GIRLS) can cook for themselves, do their own laundry, and even earn their own money.

Secret #38:

SENIORS are Also INDEPENDENT

Seniors in Canada usually live by themselves, and then may go to a Retirement or Nursing home.

SECRET #38: SENIORS' INDEPENDENCE

Another mystery to many newcomers is the way we treat our parents and grandparents. In many countries, older people are revered and catered to. They did everything for YOU when you were growing up, so now you have to do everything for THEM.

Canadian seniors, however, usually prefer to live INDEPENDENTLY; they DON'T WANT to live with their adult kids and/or grandkids. About one-third of Canadians over the age of 60 are still working (full-time or part-time). This isn't because they're too POOR to retire or because they HATE their kids, but because most Canadians don't LIKE to be DEPENDENT.

When living independently becomes impossible, often for health reasons, many seniors sell their homes and move into a Retirement Home (though this is EXPENSIVE - $1,500 to $6,000+ per month) and then, when full-time nursing care is required, into a Nursing Home (prices are regulated – approx. $2,000 to $3,000 per month).

If seniors can't afford a nursing home, there are government-subsidized nursing homes, but there is often a considerable waiting list (about 3 years in the GTA) for a bed in one of these facilities.

Secret #39:
The Nuclear Family

Most Canadian families live with only the parent(s) and their children (not with grandparents, aunts, uncles or cousins).

SECRET #39: WHAT IS 'THE NUCLEAR FAMILY'?

In many countries, people live together with parents, grandparents, and maybe aunts, uncles, and cousins. This is called the 'extended' family.

Most Canadians live in a 'nuclear' family – only the mother, father, and their children. Grandparents may live nearby or far away, but they may still be working, so it's not as common for Canadian grandparents to take care of their grandchildren while the parents work.

If you're admitted to Emergency, the only people who are allowed to visit you are 'immediate' family. This varies, not only from province to province, but also from hospital to hospital, and may include your spouse, parents and grandparents, children and grand children, brothers and sisters, mother-in-law and father- in-law, brothers-in-law and sisters-in-law, daughters-in-law and sons-in-law. Adopted, half, and step members *may* also be included in immediate family.

However, aunts, uncles, cousins, nieces and nephews are NOT considered "immediate family".

When we have a special event such as a wedding, the number of guests may be determined more by the COST than by social or family ties. A wedding reception may cost $100-$400 per person, so Canadians may only invite as many people as they have budgeted for.

Secret #40:
Lone-Parent Families

About 20% of families in Canada have only one parent living with the children. It's socially acceptable for children to live in a lone-parent family.

SECRET #40: LONE-PARENT FAMILIES

Yet another perhaps SHOCKING difference between your home country and Canada is the prevalence of lone-parent families (formerly called 'single-parent families' – which is no longer POLITE). At school events or other family-oriented events, you may be surprised to see a lot of mothers or fathers there alone. If you ask your kids, they can probably tell you which of their classmates is living with 'only Mommy' or 'only Daddy'.

50 years ago, there was a strong STIGMA attached to parenting without a partner, but it's pretty NORMAL now. Often the parents are sharing custody (see **Secret #48**), so while only ONE parent lives with the child at a time, the child still interacts with BOTH parents (equally or not).

Daycare subsidies, housing subsidies and child-support payments are three things that have helped make it possible for women to divorce men they aren't happy with; to leave possibly ABUSIVE husbands.

So, before you JUDGE a lone-parent family, you should wonder WHY that person chose to parent – at least sometimes – ALONE. Once you get to know one of these parents – ASK. I'm SURE they have a story to tell you!

Secret #41:

Sexual Relationships – the LAW:

- In Canada, the age of consent to sexual activity is 16. HOWEVER, the "close in age" rule means that:

- 12- and 13-year-olds can be sexual with people who are no more than 2 years older than them

- 14- and 15-year-olds can be sexual with people who are no more than 5 years older than them

SECRET #41: WHEN WILL KIDS START HAVING SEX?

Canadian society is, as you have probably figured out by now – pretty TOLERANT – not just of religious & cultural differences – but of EVERYONE. It's probably one of the reasons you CAME here. That DOESN'T make it EASY to accept that after about 6 months in Canada, your kids are probably going to act MORE 'Canadian' than like your home culture, and sex is a part of that (though almost NO ONE is willing to talk about it)!

I grew up on a farm, and was brought up to tell it like I see it – that sugar-coating reality doesn't CHANGE it – My dad used to say, "If you coat sh** in chocolate, it's STILL sh**!"

So forgive me for telling you that your kids may start having sex at around 15-16 years old, and that SOME kids will start at 12-13 years old!! (AND that it's LEGAL, within limits!)

Talking to kids about birth control and SAFE SEX (using CONDOMS) is an important RESPONSIBILTY for parents here. Kids are given Sex Education at school, but if you don't talk to them about sex because it's SHAMEFUL to you, your kids may be TOO ASHAMED to ask you the questions they need to ask in order to grow up SAFE & STRONG.

Secret #42:
VIRGINITY

Most Canadian kids start dating at about 15-16 years old. This MAY or may NOT be a sexual relationship, but it's NORMAL for us to have sex before marriage.

SECRET #42: VIRGINITY?

It's probably OBVIOUS from **Secret #41**, but women in Canada DON'T usually 'save themselves for marriage' (remain a virgin until married). I'm sure some do, and in the past, it was expected, but FEMINISTS noticed that NOBODY expected a MAN to wait until marriage, and decided it was therefore unfair to expect WOMEN to wait!

The logic is that for every young MAN who has sex, there is usually a WOMAN involved, so if we think if it's okay for men, it must be okay for women.

I realize that other cultures may have different values and ethics, but this is what's normal here. As I said before, we mostly talk to our kids about SAFE SEX – that is, using birth control and condoms to prevent pregnancy or sexually transmitted diseases.

If you're not comfortable talking about sex, you can call Telehealth Ontario, which is a free, confidential service you can call to get health advice or information. A Registered Nurse will take your call 24 hours a day, seven days a week. Service is available in English & French, with translators for some other languages.

Toll-free: 1-866-797-0000

Secret #43:
Dating – Getting SERIOUS

Most Canadians want to live with their love partner before getting married. We usually don't have a big party to celebrate getting engaged.

SECRET #43: GETTING SERIOUS

Most couples in Canada live together before getting married. Many of us actually believe that it's NECESSARY – because you really don't KNOW someone until you have LIVED with them!

As I said in **Secret #35**, it's quite acceptable here to live 'common law', so some couples NEVER get officially married.

When people DO decide to get married, they often set the date for the wedding 6 to 18 months in the future, because so many Canadians have family spread all over the world and it takes TIME to organize and plan for hotels and flights.

Many cultures have a BIG party to celebrate an engagement, but here, the couple may simply send out a 'Save the Date' card to announce their engagement, and then celebrate privately with their parents and siblings.

This is NOT RUDE to us (however strange it may seem to you!)

We ARE happy when our children decide to get married, though. It's a WONDERFUL event!

Secret #44:
Who PAYS for WEDDINGS?

Usually the cost is split between both sets of parents (& the engaged couple may also contribute).

SECRET #44: WHO PAYS FOR WEDDINGS?

Traditionally in Canada, the parents of the bride paid for the wedding. Like most other traditions in Canada, there has been a lot of change in the last 50 years.

Today, the cost of a wedding may be paid by either set of parents (Often, by whoever has more money), or it may be SPLIT between the parents of the bride and the parents of the groom. Sometimes, if the people getting married are both working, they will also contribute to the cost.

WHY? Well, a typical wedding in Canada costs around $25,000 to $50,000!! And that's for only 100 guests. My Pakistani friend had 400 guests at her wedding, and her parents described it as a 'small' wedding! So the cost can be considerably HIGHER than that.

Weddings in Canada can also be VERY small – as few as the bride & groom and two witnesses, or just parents and siblings.

People might get married in a place of worship (religious building), at a Wedding Chapel, a banquet hall, at home or even on the beach. If it's a large wedding, the Reception may be at a banquet hall, or else be catered.

Secret #45:

Who SHOULDN'T you INVITE to a Wedding?

We usually invite close family & friends. The bride & groom may invite colleagues but NOT their boss.

SECRET #45: WHO SHOULDN'T YOU INVITE?

My ESL students told me that it's common in their home country to invite ALL of your colleagues or classmates, as well as your BOSS, to a family wedding. This gave me CULTURE SHOCK!

Maybe because we are CHEAP (see **Secret #16**), we DON'T usually invite colleagues or classmates, and we DEFINITELY DON'T invite our boss! The bride and groom may invite colleagues who are also friends, as well as their colleagues' spouses, but NOT those people's parents – or kids.

Former classmates who have stayed in touch, and are considered CLOSE FRIENDS might be invited, but NOT our whole graduating class!

KIDS are NOT automatically invited if YOU are! (Often, kids are invited to the Reception but not the Ceremony.) Check with the bride & groom to clarify.

I think besides it being EXPENSIVE for the people who are paying for the wedding, the issue is ALSO that weddings are EXPENSIVE for the people you invite. If you invite me to your son or daughter's wedding, I need to buy a gift ($100-$200 or MORE), as well as get an appropriate dress and shoes. Weddings vary in formality a LOT – I have been to weddings where people wore BLUE JEANS! – but usually, we are expected to wear semi-formal clothing.

Secret #46:
Same-Sex PARENTS

Most Canadians accept same-sex couples, and same-sex couples can adopt children or use a surrogate to have a child.

SECRET #46: SAME-SEX PARENTING

For many of my immigrant ESL students, one of the most CHALLENGING aspects of Canadian culture to understand is our acceptance of people being gay. I explained LGBTQ orientations in **Secret #5**, but I'd like to explain about same-sex PARENTS.

Gay couples can adopt children, or have a SURROGATE have a baby for them. Your child may have friends with 'two Mommies' or 'two Daddies'. We accept this as NORMAL.

For many Canadians, same-sex parenting may still be a bit strange, too, but if Canada is going to support EQUALITY, we have to support DIVERSITY.

You may meet same-sex parents at school events, birthday parties, weddings, and other public celebrations.

A gay man will introduce you to his husband (or 'partner'), and a gay woman will introduce you to her wife (or 'partner'). PLEASE treat them with the SAME COURTESY and RESPECT as ANY other couple!

Thank you.

Secret #47:
DIVORCE is Common

About 38% of marriages in Canada end in divorce. It's socially acceptable to be divorced, and for children to have divorced parents.

SECRET #47: DIVORCE

If you and your spouse separate and then maintain separate residences for one year, you can apply for a 'no fault' divorce – which means you don't have to go to court to provide a REASON for your divorce. Since more than 1/3 of all marriages in Canada end in divorce (and the percent goes UP for 2nd and 3rd marriages!), it's become commonplace to socialize with people who are either divorced or remarried.

50 years ago, this was not the case. People in Canada stayed married, usually for life, happily or unhappily. Then, along came Women's Liberation, Daycare and Child Support, and women suddenly had more OPTIONS. Domestic Abuse and Infidelity were no longer tolerated. Women went back into the workforce and earned independent incomes.

When my ESL students ask me why Canadians get divorced, I answer, "Because we CAN." It is socially acceptable and financially feasible. A divorced man or woman, with or without children, can find another mate. You don't have to live alone, in shame, for the rest of your life, just because your marriage didn't work out.

To me, we divorce for the same reason we get married – because we want to be HAPPY.

Secret #48:
JOINT CUSTODY

After divorce, it's common for parents to have Joint Custody. They share time with the kids 50/50.

SECRET #48: JOINT CUSTODY

If you DO get divorced, most couples choose to share time with the children, 50/50. This is called Joint Custody. Children may spend one week with Mom, and the next with Dad. At the recommendation of our marriage counsellor, my ex-husband and I alternated having the children 2 days each (and 3 days on the weekend). My ex took our sons camping for 2 weeks each summer.

Some parents want Full Custody – which is a legal term, meaning the children live full-time with one parent, while the other parent has Visitation Rights (typically, every Saturday or every other weekend).

Regardless of Joint Custody or Full Custody, the parent earning more money usually has to pay Child Support (see **Secret #49).** Exes also share bigger expenses, such as lessons, sports fees, and dental or medical bills.

Child Support amounts and the division of expenses are usually laid out in a SEPARATION AGREEMENT, which is *negotiated when the couple separates, NOT when they get a divorce.*

Secret #49:
CHILD SUPPORT

The parent who earns more money (usually the father) pays money to his Ex each month for the children's expenses. This is the LAW.

SECRET #49: CHILD SUPPORT

If you do get a divorce, you are often dividing your assets in half, and losing the income of your spouse. For many women, that means moving toward (or even INTO) living in POVERTY. Women simply DON'T earn as much as men (see **Secret #81**), so losing your husband's income means, for most women, a lower standard of living.

Because of this, our laws provide for Child Support – money paid by the higher-earning spouse (usually the man) to the lower-earning spouse. You can calculate the approximate amount of child support due using our government Child Support Calculator (Google: Canada child support calculator)

Some people think that women are getting 'rich' off of child support. According to some research, it costs about $13,000 per year to raise a child in Canada (and that's an AVERAGE. Daycare costs ALONE in the GTA are about $1,600 per month!)

Paying child support is NOT OPTIONAL. If you neglect to (or REFUSE to) pay, you can go to JAIL.

Secret #50:
Do we REALLY 'share' the Kids?

Yes, we DO. It's common for BOTH divorced parents to go to school meetings, as well as important events such as their child's graduation or wedding.

SECRET #50: HANGING OUT WITH YOUR EX

After divorce, after you get through the ugly haggling over division of assets, custody and child support, you have to 'make nice' with your ex because BOTH of you will probably be attending school meetings and events, as well as your children's graduations, weddings and other celebrations.

Believe it or not, thanks to our super-POLITE society, many exes get along quite well! We may HATE each other, but we both want what's BEST for our children. And if that means SMILING at your ex and their new spouse (and maybe their new FAMILY) at social functions, then that's what you should do (if you can!).

My ex and I wrote into our Separation Agreement that neither of us could move more than 15 km away from the other, so that the children could always attend the same school, regardless of which parent they were staying with. This placed restrictions on the jobs we could take, the relationships we could have, and the housing choices we had.

But we did it for the KIDS. Maybe we couldn't stay married, but we wanted to minimize the stress on the children.

Secret #51:
"ME" time

Even when the parents AREN'T divorced, it's normal for the father to take care of the children for a few hours each week so his wife has time to herself.

SECRET #51: "ME" TIME

I realize that I'm going to make some people ANGRY with a LOT of these secrets, and I understand that it sounds SEXIST to say that dads 'take care of' the children, as if those children aren't THEIRS as well.

But I'm trying to talk about the SECRET stuff, the stuff most Canadians can't – or won't – tell you. And the TRUTH is that child care is still MORE the wife's responsibility than the husband's. Of course, there are EXCEPTIONS to this rule, but RESEARCH shows that women are still the primary caregivers for both children and elderly parents.

Luckily, in many 'modern' families, GOOD husbands will take the children out to the park or the mall for a few hours on a Saturday or Sunday, so the wife can have a few hours of "ME Time" to herself. (HINT, HINT!!)

During this time, a woman might get a haircut or get her nails done; she might read a book or go shopping; or she might just take a NAP (like *I* did!)

Secret #52:
How to SUCCEED at School

Canadian teachers expect children to do 25% MORE than is required. That "extra effort" is what gets a 4/4 on assignments.

SECRET #52: THE CANADIAN "WORK ETHIC"

My ESL students are confused when they see the marks on their children's homework and assignments. Their children have done EVERYTHING the teacher (or rubric) asked them to do, and they may have done it 100% RIGHT, and they STILL only get a mark of 3/4 (75%)!! What's UP with THAT?

Well, another unwritten rule in Canada is related to our strong Work Ethic. If you want your child to get 4/4, they need to do 25% MORE than is required! Even when my kids were in Grade 1, they handed in their homework inside a plastic report cover (from the Dollar store), with a Title Page including the teacher's name, their name, and the date. If the teacher asked for 4 references, we gave him/her 5. (You get the idea.)

This DOESN'T mean writing a 6-page report when the teacher asked for a 4-page report, though! Teachers don't want to read a longer report.

This applies at WORK, too. I always contribute MORE than is in my job description! In many countries, if there are no customers, a clerk can sit and chat with other workers or read a book. Here, if there are no customers, CLEAN SOMETHING!

Secret #53:
ACTIVE Learning

The Canadian school system focuses on teaching kids HOW to LEARN rather than on teaching FACTS. Kids are expected to work INDEPENDENTLY.

SECRET #53: JUST WHAT IS "ACTIVE LEARNING"?

In many countries, the style of teaching and learning is what we call 'rote' learning, where the teachers present FACTS which the students WRITE DOWN and MEMORIZE, and then regurgitate for tests and exams. Students are expected to SHUT UP, LISTEN, and NOT ask questions!

This makes life EASIER for teachers, but often does NOT produce learners that adapt easily to new situations or have the ability to IMPROVISE SOLUTIONS.

Canadian educators, on the other hand, changed the focus in schools from learning FACTS to "learning how to learn" – ACTIVE learning. Children are given a basic lesson on a topic, and then are presented with a CHALLENGE where they need to FIGURE OUT how to solve the problem. This builds STRATEGIES for LEARNING NEW SKILLS that will benefit children throughout school and their adult lives.

This means that while Canadian kids may not do as well in Math and Science tests as children in many other countries, we EXCEL in INNOVATION & INVENTION.

Secret #54:
YOU'RE a TEACHER, too

Parents are expected to supervise their children's homework & assignments, and to HELP the child to complete them CORRECTLY. If you can't, you should hire a TUTOR.

SECRET #54: WHY YOU HAVE TO BE A TEACHER

Connected to the idea of Active Learning is the idea that parents are PARTNERS with TEACHERS in educating children. If your child's report card says, "_____ needs to take more care to make sure homework is completed correctly and on time", this is as much as criticism of YOU as your child!

You are expected to HELP your child with his/her homework and assignments, including internet research and other projects. If your child is struggling in school, and you can't help, you should hire a tutor.

It helps if you can figure out your child's Learning Style. My first two sons were visual/kinesthetic learners, so they learned best by looking at something and COPYING it, or by DOING something. (Cooking is GREAT for teaching FRACTIONS and MEASURING!)

My 3rd son didn't respond well to the methods that had worked with the first two, but I eventually figured out that he's an auditory learner. He needed to LISTEN & REPEAT things out LOUD in order to remember them.

Secret #55:

COMMUNICATE with the TEACHER

Parents are expected to keep in touch with the teacher. If he/she emails you, ALWAYS respond, if only to say, "Got it" or "Thank you."

SECRET #55: COMMUNICATING WITH THE TEACHER

We'll dive more deeply into emails in **Secret #76**, but it's important to know that you should ALWAYS respond to emails from the school (unless it's an email blast with a noreply@abcschool.ca address).

Responding to emails is an IMPORTANT sign that you accept your responsibility as a PARTNER in your child's Education (and it's just POLITE in general to let people know that you DID receive the email), so you should email back at least, "Thanks."

If the email was general information on your child's class or their progress, you should say, "Thanks for the update." If they're letting you know that there was an issue with your child that day, you should say, "Thanks for letting me know. Is there anything we need to do?"

REGISTER: (How **FORMAL** or **INFORMAL** should you be?) This is another good topic to Google:

social register in communications in Canada

In general, though, you should use the same register as the person who emails you. If the teacher signs her name, "Mrs. Mills", you should write, "Dear Mrs. Mills" (but ONLY the 1st time! – use "Hi Mrs. Mills" thereafter. If she signs, "Diane Mills", write, "Dear Diane" and sign your FIRST name.

"

Secret #56:
Understanding
REPORT CARDS

Your child's report card tells you about both their academic & their social or work-habit progress. These are considered EQUALLY IMPORTANT.

SECRET #56: REPORT CARD JARGON

Even if you were BORN in Canada, report cards are DIFFICULT to understand. One of the reasons for this is that teachers in Canada aren't really allowed to say BAD things about your child, so if there are issues, they need to be expressed in INDIRECT LANGUAGE. *Indirect language in Canada* is ANOTHER subject you can Google, but here's a fairly simple 'translation' of some of the jargon you might see on your child's report card:

4 = EXCELLENT What teachers WANT (75-100%)	3 = GOOD (but NOT ENOUGH) 50-75%	2 = BARELY ACCEPTABLE- 50%	1 = FAILING <50%
is able to _____ **INDEPEDENTLY**	*is able to* _____	is able to _____ **BUT**	tends to *AVOID* _____... **requires ASSISTANCE** in order to _____
CONSISTENTLY	*Generally* able to …	… is **IMPROVING**	requires 1-to-1 **ASSISTANCE** in …
SUCCESSFULLY	…. **Somewhat successfully**	is **SOMETIMES** able to …	**UNDERESTIMATES** his/her **abilities**
CONFIDENTLY	… with **SOME** self-confidence	… with **INCREASING** confidence	**LACKS CONFIDENCE** in his/her **abilities**
EFFECTIVELY	*is able to* _____	… with **ASSISTANCE**, is able to ….	can … **WITH DIRECT ASSISTANCE**

You can see that Canadian teachers are looking for your child to work INDEPENDENTLY, CONFIDENTLY and CONSISTENTLY. None of these are necessarily about how SMART your child is. They are evaluating EQUALLY your child's ACADEMIC progress and their SOCIAL SKILLS and WORK HABITS.

Secret #57:
HOMEWORK

Some Canadian children don't get ANY homework, and some get TOO MUCH. About 10 minutes per grade is considered normal (i.e., a Grade 5 student should do 50 minutes per day).

SECRET #57: YOU CAN ASSIGN HOMEWORK, TOO

This may be the ONLY way to guarantee your child gets an excellent education! When my kids didn't bring home any homework, I made them do one unit in one of the "SMART" workbooks (EnglishSMART, MathSMART, etc.) – for the grade BELOW the one they were in.

For example, when my son was in Grade 3, he would work in the _GRADE 2_ book (These books are based on the Ontario Curriculum, and provide a good review of rules and some simple exercises.) Some of the things in the Grade 3 book were things he hadn't studied yet, and I wanted to ensure each child had a SOLID understanding of each subject. The books go up to Grade 12!

This next thing is a PARENTING secret rather than a Canadian secret, I think: I made my kids do their homework at the kitchen table, and I tried to ALWAYS sit with them while they did it. I wanted them to do it themselves if they could, but I also wanted to show them that I was INTERESTED in what they were doing and AVAILABLE to help.

It's HARD to focus on Homework if Mom or Dad is off watching TV in the other room! You can read an ESL book (see **Secret #59**) or write emails, but don't play games on your screen (That's ALSO torture for the kids!).

Secret #58:
Get INVOLVED in your child's SCHOOL

If you can, VOLUNTEER at your child's school. You are also expected to attend ALL school functions (in Elementary School).

SECRET #58: GET INVOLVED WITH THEIR SCHOOL

If you have time, offer to volunteer – either some time each week in your child's class – or on a casual basis as a volunteer when there are FIELD TRIPS. This not only demonstrates your commitment to your child, but offers you a chance to learn how your child is learning, how he/she gets along with classmates, and what our "school culture" is like. Schools here might be VERY different from the kind of school you went to!

At least ONE parent (but preferably BOTH parents) should attend school functions and celebrations. You may have to take time off work to do it, but it will make your child feel treasured, and confirms with the school that you CARE about your child.

Go to the "Meet the Teacher" nights – up until High School, anyway – (even if you're SHY about your English; REMEMBER, immigrant parents are COMMON here!) and go to the REPORT CARD meeting. Introduce yourself with ONLY your FIRST name (it sounds FRIENDLIER – and many Canadians have trouble pronouncing foreign names!)

If you have a concern about your child, you can ask for a meeting with your child's teacher ANYTIME. Email or call to make an appointment.

Secret #59:
You need to learn PHRASAL VERBS

Spoken English is FULL of idioms & phrasal verbs, and the faster you learn them, the faster you'll understand us.

SECRET #59: IDIOMS & PHRASAL VERBS

If you've studied English, you know that our SPOKEN language is quite DIFFERENT from our WRITTEN language. Spoken sentences are shorter and simpler in general, but they're also full of idioms, phrasal verbs and slang.

For example, you can understand EACH of the WORDS in "look forward to" something – WITHOUT UNDERSTANDING that TOGETHER, they mean, "anticipate happily".

That's why a Spanish speaker can understand a LOT of WRITTEN English (because it contains many Latin-based words, similar to Spanish, French, Italian and Romanian), but will often get LOST trying to understand us when we SPEAK.

TAKE THE TIME to LEARN phrasal verbs and idioms. Your listening comprehension will go up in direct proportion to your study!

I recommend getting these 2 books (And they're NOT paying me to say so!):

1. Phrasal Verbs (Barron's ESL Proficiency)

by Carl W. Hart

2. A Year in the Life of an ESL Student

by Edward J. Francis

Secret #60:

Adult Education: WHY do I need a CERTIFICATE?

Canadian employers DON'T TRUST resumes, so they depend on independent (Canadian) certificates to confirm your skills.

SECRET #60: WHY DO I NEED A "CANADIAN" CERTIFICATE?

Finding a job in Canada may be COMPLETELY different from finding a job in your home country (see **Secret #62**). One of the differences is that even if you have an EXCELLENT education and LOTS of experience, even if you CAME here because you qualified as a Skilled Worker, Canadian employers are going to be SUSPICIOUS of your claims.

This ISN'T necessarily a form of PREJUDICE – they demand PROOF from Canadians BORN here, too! This is because many people LIE on their resumes. They claim to have a certain education or certain skills, but many employers have been BURNED by hiring people (based on their GREAT resumes) who turned out to be INCOMPETENT. Many employers give candidates a TEST as part of the interview process.

So these days, you need independent PROOF that what you say about yourself is TRUE. A degree or diploma from your home country is hard for a Canadian employer to evaluate (even if it's in English!) Here, we know which schools are GOOD and which ones AREN'T. We don't really know this about schools in other countries.

Therefore, as soon as you can, take a course to update your skills and get a CANADIAN certificate. Things change in every occupation, and updating skills is VERY important here (see **Secret #61**).

Secret #61:
LIFELONG LEARNING

Canadians are SERIOUS about keeping our skills up to date. You are expected to do Professional Development activities every YEAR.

SECRET #61: MORE SCHOOL – WHY??

"Lifelong Learning" is a KEY value in the Canadian workplace. Especially since almost EVERY job involves using some form of TECHNOLOGY, it's important that we keep up with changes in that technology.

The regulations, rules, or laws for various occupations also change and evolve, year by year, so we do 'professional development' (PD) workshops (training that could be from a couple of hours to weeks long!) in order to update and improve our skills for our jobs. Usually, PD is paid for by the company and you are paid your wage while you do it, so it's not ALL bad!

More and more PD takes place through Computer-Based Training (CBT), so don't be surprised if your boss tells you that you must complete some CBT.

ABBREVIATIONS are part of the JARGON you need to learn for your occupation. Every job has them! (see **Secret #72**) When I'm speaking to another teacher, I can tell her, "I'm doing PBLA to confirm the CLBs of my LINC students" and she will understand me perfectly!

PD will often give you NEW CERTIFICATIONS to add to your resume, too!

Secret #62:
Finding a Job is DIFFERENT Here

You need HELP finding a job here. Resumes, cover letters & interviews need to be "Canadian" style. Luckily, there are MANY free centres to help you!

SECRET #62: FINDING A JOB IN CANADA

Many newcomers, even VERY qualified ones, have a VERY hard time landing their first job in Canada. Part of the reason for this is that we have a number of "governing bodies" for our major professions – doctors, dentists, lawyers, engineers, accountants, etc. – that have stringent rules for practicing these professions here (see **Secret #60**).

The OTHER reason, though, is that resumes, cover letters, interviews and JOB SEARCH are ALL VERY DIFFERENT here! They're even different between one occupation and another! If you send a "bank" resume for a "teaching" job, or vice-versa, you will probably NEVER get an interview.

Luckily, the Canadian government sponsors MANY different organizations to help citizens and newcomers to find work, and it's a FREE service. If you are qualified to work in Canada (However, ONLY if you are unemployed or work fewer than 20 hours per week), these organizations can help you learn the "Canadian styles" of resume, cover letters, interviews and job search.

Google: Find a job - Canada.ca

to find an employment assistance centre near you.

Secret #63:
VOLUNTEER

Volunteering is GOOD for Canada, and gives you a JOB REFERENCE to prove you are Punctual, Dependable and FRIENDLY.

SECRET #63: WHY YOU SHOULD VOLUNTEER

If you're looking for a job, the most IMPORTANT thing to know about VOLUNTEER WORK in Canada is that employers VALUE volunteer work almost EQUAL to PAID work! (Especially when it comes to that slippery demand for "Canadian Experience" or "Canadian References".)

Employers who want references are looking to CONFIRM 3 things about you:

1.   You are PUNCTUAL. You show up 10-15 minutes EARLY. You come back from breaks or lunch ON TIME.

2.   You are DEPENDABLE. It's VITAL that you treat volunteer work AS IF it were a REAL JOB. If you're sick, call them and TELL them why you can't come in. If you SAY you'll do something, DO it. **Don't think**, "Hey! They're not PAYING me! So it doesn't really MATTER if I do it or not!"

3.   You are FRIENDLY (with coworkers and customers). You could have the BEST skills in the world, but if you're difficult to get along with, nobody wants to work with you!

Your volunteer work HELPS Canada, and provides you with a GOOD REFERENCE for a job, so you need to treat volunteer work AS SERIOUSLY AS paid work!

Secret #64:
BUILD your NETWORK

About 70% of Canadians find jobs through their network (friends, family & colleagues). Find a group through meetup.com

SECRET #64: BUILDING A NETWORK

You probably had a network of friends, family, neighbours, coworkers and former colleagues in your home country – people who could help you find a job. It's hard to leave that behind and start from scratch (zero) here.

There are a number of places to look for contacts that can be a part of your network. Make sure to have a profile on *LinkedIn.com* If you join *meetup.com* for FREE, you can probably find a local group of people with similar interests. They also have business networking groups, and business owners groups. It's free to JOIN, but individual meetings may charge a small fee to cover the rental of the room where you meet.

Getting that Canadian CERTIFICATE (see **Secret #60**) will also give you a chance to meet some new people, and your instructor MIGHT be able to help you find a job.

Google: *ENHANCED LANGUAGE TRAINING* programs can not only give you more clues about adapting to Canadian Workplace Culture, but will also help you with resumes, cover letters, etc.

If you aren't a CONFIDENT speaker (see **Secret #65**), I recommend joining TOASTMASTERS (Google it). It's NOT FREE, but WELL worth the money.

Secret #65:
Show SELF-CONFIDENCE

In Canada, we EXPECT you to be PROUD of your accomplishments. Practice speaking confidently about yourself. "Humble" is not really valued here.

SECRET #65: YOU SHOULD SHOW SELF-CONFIDENCE

One of the BIGGEST challenges that my ESL students have told me about is the need to BRAG about yourself in job interviews.

It's NOT really 'bragging' – bragging is NEGATIVE. What I'm talking about is speaking CONFIDENTLY about yourself and your skills. Many Canadian employers equate 'confident' with 'skilled'. As anyone who has seen American Idol can TELL you, this is NOT always TRUE!!

Nevertheless, a typical interview question will be, "Why should we hire YOU and not one of the other candidates?" If you are HUMBLE (as you were EXPECTED to be in your home country), you probably WON'T get the job.

You should practice what we call your "elevator speech" – a 1 to 2 minute description of your best qualities and skills – (What would an Advertisement about you say?) – What you'd want to tell a potential employer if you found yourself on an elevator with him/her for JUST a couple of minutes. You don't need to go CRAZY!

Just say something like, "With my Master's degree in Engineering, and 14 years' experience in power production, I think I can handle just about ANY project you could throw at me."

Secret #66:
Get PAID for Statutory Holidays

We have different Official holidays in each province, where an employer MUST pay you for that day if you were scheduled to work that day. FIND OUT what they are, because some employers will try not to pay you!

SECRET #66: DON'T LET EMPLOYERS *CHEAT* YOU

Canada has only 2 Statutory (legal) Holidays that are Christian – Christmas and Easter. All of our other holidays and festivals are secular (and MANY Canadians celebrate Christmas and Easter as secular holidays as well).

It's important to find out which are the Statutory Holidays in your province or territory, because those are the days where employers MUST pay you if you were scheduled to work that day, but the business is closed for the holiday.

Unfortunately, some employers in Canada will take advantage of your ignorance, and won't pay you for the holiday unless you 'remind' them that they MUST pay you for it. If you are an hourly employee and asked to work on a statutory holiday, the employer MUST pay you "time and a half" – that is, your wage x 1.5 per hour. So, if you normally earn $20/hr, you'd be paid $30/hr to work on that holiday.

We have other special days, such as Valentine's Day, Mother's Day, Father's Day, and Remembrance Day, that are celebrated by most Canadians, but are NOT statutory holidays, so businesses stay open on those days.

Secret #67:
Embrace DIVERSITY

Prejudice and bigotry are NOT acceptable here. Your coworkers will be from ALL races, creeds & colours. Show RESPECT to EVERYONE.

SECRET #67: DIVERSITY AT WORK

GREAT! You got the job! When you arrive at work on your first day, though, you may find that you are the ONLY 'foreign-trained' person there, or you may find that you are one of MANY diverse groups. Some people call their workplace 'the United Nations'!

Some of your coworkers might even be from a group that you were brought up to fear or despise. This is where the TOLERANCE & RESPECT aspect of Canadian culture becomes CRUCIAL to your success.

Many workplaces have a Zero Tolerance policy for workplace harassment or discrimination. If a coworker or customer feels that you are not treating him/her with respect and courtesy, they can report you to your manager or Human Resources (HR) and you can be FIRED on the SPOT. The SAME protections apply to YOU. (see **Secret #83**)

If you have never met someone who is VERY different from you – a Sikh or a Hijabi, for instance – it's absolutely OKAY to ask them about what they're wearing (at break or lunchtime). MOST people are HAPPY to explain their culture or a religious practice, as long as you are RESPECTFUL & FRIENDLY when you ask about it.

Secret #68:
ASK QUESTIONS at Work

Speaking up in MEETINGS, offering opinions & asking questions will help get you a PROMOTION in Canada.

SECRET #68: PARTICIPATE IN MEETINGS

In many countries, when the boss or supervisor SPEAKS at meetings, their subordinates should LISTEN, quietly and respectfully. You should do that HERE, too!

The DIFFERENCE is, that when the boss says, "Any questions?" you are expected to ASK your question in front of everyone else, even if you think it might be a "dumb" question. If the boss asks, "Any suggestions?" EVERYONE in the room is WELCOME to participate and make suggestions.

It doesn't mean they're going to ACT on your suggestion, necessarily. But Canadian employers are always looking for LEADERS, and leaders are the ones who get PROMOTED!

This DOESN'T mean you should talk, and talk, and TALK! Pay attention to the people around you. We have a saying: "When in Rome, do as the Romans do." This means that when you're not sure of the social rules in a given situation, you should emulate the behaviour of the people around you. This is especially true in meetings at work!

Oh – and *SMILE!* (- unless the topic is SERIOUS.)

Secret #69:
Arrive EARLY

You should arrive 10-15 minutes BEFORE you're scheduled to start work. Use this time to get coffee, go to the washroom, and say hello to your coworkers. Being late can get you FIRED.

SECRET #69: BE "ON TIME"

Many countries have quite a relaxed attitude toward schedules and appointments. Canada is NOT one of them!

If you have a doctor or dentist appointment, and you are 15 minutes late, the appointment will probably be CANCELLED, and you may be CHARGED ($50-$100) for the missed visit.

In Canada, we expect you to arrive 10 or 15 minutes EARLY for ANY job, business meeting or appointment. It's a GREAT time to engage in a bit of Small Talk (see **Secret #8**) with your coworkers. Before the time you are scheduled to START work, you should boot up your computer if you're using one, use the washroom, and get your coffee.

One of my ESL students, who was also working full time, told me she usually arrived at work at about 9:15 a.m. "So, you're essentially HALF an hour LATE!" I told her. "Well, I work until 5:30, so that time is made up at the end of the day," she argued.

"That doesn't COUNT." I said. "Your employer is ONLY going to notice that you ARRIVE late, NOT that you WORK late!"

Being LATE 3 times can get you FIRED.

Secret #70:
Be DEPENDABLE

Don't LIE. If you SAY you'll do something, DO it! If you can't do it, ask for Help. Never say "Yes" to something you absolutely CAN'T do.

SECRET #70: BE DEPENDABLE

Another strong value in Canadian culture is being DEPENDABLE. This means being HONEST, TRUSTWORTHY, and RELIABLE.

It means that if you SAY you will do something, DO it. Telling your boss that you can do something, so that he/she doesn't find out that you CAN'T do it, is going to get you in TROUBLE. You are better off to admit that you need help.

However, DON'T say, "I CAN'T do it." Say, "I'm not sure how to do that. Is there someone I can ask for help or guidance?" This is perfectly acceptable, especially when you are learning a new job. Canadian employers are NOT GREAT at offering TRAINING before you start. They usually expect you to learn 'on the job', so asking for help is NORMAL.

Also, DON'T make promises you can't keep. DON'T say, "I'll have it done by Friday" if you know you WON'T. We tend to take people at their word, so if you SAID Friday, that means we EXPECT it FRIDAY!

In general, TELL the TRUTH at work. HONESTY is VERY important to us. If you ARE late getting to work, just say, "Sorry I'm late." Don't make up an EXCUSE, because no one will BELIEVE it, anyway. We even have a JOKE about excuses – "My grandmother died AGAIN."

Secret #71:
RESPECT your BOSS

We are often very FRIENDLY with our superiors at work, but we must ALWAYS show them RESPECT. Don't talk badly about them (even after you LEAVE the company).

SECRET #71: RESPECTING THE BOSS

You may not NEED this Secret at ALL. I think people in MOST countries must respect their supervisor, manager, or boss.

What CAN be CONFUSING, though, is the level of INFORMALITY we practice at work. I call my supervisor by her first name; I call HER manager by her first name; I call the CEO of our whole organization by HER first name! With everyone using first names, it's easy to mistake that friendliness to mean we are EQUALS, and that I can treat my boss the same as a FRIEND.

This is NOT TRUE. Even though we call almost everyone by their first name, we MUST obey our supervisor or manager's instructions and requests, and we should NEVER speak badly about them, even after we LEAVE the company!

To "climb the corporate ladder" in Canada is NOT as straightforward as in many other countries. Your own company may ignore you when hiring for a position that you are well-qualified for. You may need to get your promotion by taking a higher job with ANOTHER COMPANY.

One or two years later, you might get ANOTHER PROMOTION by going BACK to the FIRST company. So NEVER speak badly about your BOSS!

Secret #72:
Learn the JARGON

Every job has its own unique VOCABULARY. Learn it and use it. Be as FORMAL or INFORMAL as your coworkers.

SECRET #72: LEARN THE JARGON!

In **Secret #61**, I mentioned that you need to learn the occupation-specific language – the "JARGON" – for your job, including the ABBREVIATIONS that are common.

If you are looking for a job here, you should learn the jargon and its abbreviations BEFORE the job interview! How? Google *"vocabulary for _____"* (name of occupation). Most occupations have websites that offer a *GLOSSARY* of common terms for their occupation.

Part of speaking confidently is being able to use the jargon for that occupation. You DON'T want to go into an engineering interview and have the interviewer ask you, "What experience do you have writing programming for the OWS and the EWS? Are you familiar with the DCS screens?" – and have NO IDEA what he/she just asked!!

I think jargon serves 2 purposes: the first is overt – it's a kind of short-form which allows speakers with common experiences and knowledge to express complex ideas quickly.

The 2nd purpose is covert – it keeps people who are NOT part of your "in" group from understanding what you are talking about. It makes you part of a knowledge "club".

Secret #73:
OBEY the RULES

As we do when driving, most Canadians respect the RULES at work. If the rules aren't CLEAR, ask your coworkers or boss to EXPLAIN.

SECRET #73: OBEYING THE RULES

My ESL students often tell me that they had Culture Shock when they started driving in Canada, because most drivers here OBEY THE DRIVING LAWS!

I tell THEM that one of MY first experiences of Culture Shock came during my TESL training (learning to be an ESL instructor). Our professor told us that we MUST WARN our students from Central and South America NOT to BRIBE a police officer who stopped them for speeding!

My professor ALSO told us to warn our students NOT to allow their friends and family to SHOPLIFT if they work in a store. She told us that in many developing countries where people aren't paid a living wage, the way they survive is to allow each other to steal from their workplace. Doing either of those things HERE may lead to JAIL time.

That means obeying the RULES at work, too. If you are told not to use your computer for personal email, Facebook, or entertainment, DON'T do it. The I.T. department routinely checks your internet usage, and if you're caught doing any of the above, you could be FIRED on the SPOT.

Secret #74:
FIND a MENTOR

If you want to get promoted in your career, it's a good idea to find an experienced person to guide you. You can ask him or her to "mentor" you.

SECRET #74: FINDING A MENTOR

With so many things to learn about how to adapt to Canadian culture and particularly to Canadian WORKPLACE culture, it's a good idea to find a MENTOR if you can.

This is an experienced worker who shows interest in you and is helpful in teaching you things. This person can be a BIG help in your career as long as you are RESPECTFUL and GRATEFUL to that person.

Tell him/her something like, "I need some guidance in developing my career in Canada. Would you be willing to mentor me? We could meet for coffee maybe once a month for me to ask questions or for you to make suggestions based on my performance at work."

Most Canadians would be flattered that you asked and might enjoy the role of guide. Some people, though, already have "too much on their plate" (too many responsibilities, not enough time) and may politely tell you "No" for this reason.

If they say Yes, set up a schedule (be FLEXIBLE about fitting into THEIR availability!) to get together once a month. If they say No, say, "That's okay. Thanks anyway. Do you know of anyone else who might be able to mentor me?"

Secret #75:

HELP Your Coworkers Understand YOUR Culture, too

During breaks or at lunchtime, share some celebrations from your culture or religion.

SECRET #75: INTRODUCE YOUR CULTURE

Your coworkers might find your clothing or your lunch food strange, but they'll probably be too polite to say anything. Canadians try to avoid bringing FISH or anything GARLICKY for our lunch. (Some workplaces BAN heating fish in the microwave!) In case you hadn't noticed, we're sensitive about strong smells.

If you've gotten friendly with one or more of your colleagues, and regularly eat lunch with them, this can be a perfect opportunity to share a BIT about your culture (NO LECTURES or SLIDE SHOWS. It's LUNCHTIME, NOT university!)

Also be aware that Canadians are mostly VERY touchy about talking about their religion (see **Secret #9** – TABOO subjects), so you CAN'T ASK us about our religion, and we DON'T like you telling us how YOUR religion is the BEST one in the WORLD. You can say, for example, "I'm Hindu, and today is Diwali – our Festival of Lights." They will probably ask questions about it and you can tell them how you and your family celebrate this festival.

Or you might explain a bit about Ramadan, or other events important to you. Just be careful not to be seen as PREACHING.

Secret #76:
Email: K.I.S.S.

In business communications, we expect you to Keep It Short & Sweet.
That means that you should tell us DIRECTLY but POLITELY what you want or need from us.

SECRET #76: K.I.S.S.

I've come across two opposite problems when dealing with emails from immigrants. One group is so DIRECT that they appear RUDE. If I ask them a question, they might respond, "I don't know" or "That's not my job" – which may both be TRUE, but aren't polite here. You should respond, "I'm not sure. Maybe you could ask _____?" (a person more qualified to answer the question).

The 2nd issue I've had is when immigrants send me EXTREMELY "flowery" emails, asking about my health, my family's health, and taking ONE PARAGRAPH to say "Hello".

Especially in BUSINESS emails, we want you to Keep it Short & Sweet. "SHORT" means, no small talk questions. Tell me what you want. "SWEET" means, be polite about it. If you have something social to say to me, put it at the END of the email. IF I have TIME, I can read and respond to the social part of your message.

You might email your colleague something like this:

Hi, Walid. I'm wondering if you can send me the report on the ABCD Project by this Friday.

BTW, how was your vacation?

Thanks,
_____ (your FIRST name)

Secret #77:
Telephone ETIQUETTE

The SAME as email, once we've said hello, we expect you to tell us DIRECTLY but POLITELY what you want or need from us.

SECRET #77: TELEPHONE ETIQUETTE

We have SO many rules about *telephone etiquette in Canada* that you should probably Google it. But here are the BASICS for HOME & WORK:

If you're calling my home, but I don't answer, you ask, "Is <u>Kate</u> there?" Once I am on the phone, you say, "Hi, <u>Kate</u>. This is _____. (your name)"

DON'T ASK ME how I am! I'll say, "Hi, _____. Can I help you?" You should IMMEDIATELY tell me the reason for your call. In other cultures, this would be extremely RUDE, but it's the social norm here. If you just want to chat, you say, "Hi, <u>Kate</u>. Have you got a minute to chat?"

If you're calling me at my school/business, and I don't answer the phone, you ask, "Can I speak to <u>Kate</u>, please?" The receptionist will say either, "One moment, I'll put you through to her" (if I'm available) or "Sorry, <u>Kate</u> isn't available right now. Can I take a message?"

If I'm available, I'll answer the phone, "<u>Kate</u> speaking. Can I help you?" and again, you should get to the point without much small talk.

Say "Okay …" or "Well …" to signal the call is ending. If we're in a HURRY, we may cut the conversation short, and this is NOT considered RUDE here.

Actually, the same rule applies FACE to FACE!

Secret #78:
Start a BUSINESS

There are many supports available to help you start a business in Canada.

Google: *Starting a business Canada*

SECRET #78: BE AN ENTREPRENEUR!

You may be DISAPPOINTED that it's HARDER to adapt to Canadian culture – or to find a job – than you imagined it would be before you came here. I'm very SORRY that there appear to be so many BARRIERS to success in Canada.

The GOOD news, though, is that Canada still IS "The Land of Opportunity", where you can arrive with NOTHING and become a SUCCESS.

Google: ***Toronto Raptor's "Super Fan", Nav Bhatia***

The Canadian government strongly supports people who have INVENTED something or want to START A BUSINESS. There are startup loans and business mentors available in most urban centres.

Check out the website on the previous page for links to the programs available as well as locations of the support organizations which might be available in your city.

Low-cost business cards can be ordered from **vistaprint.ca**

You can make a well-designed website for FREE on **wix.com**

Secret #79:

Doing Business: is a HANDSHAKE a Legal CONTRACT?

YES it IS. The Supreme Court of Canada says that a "handshake contract" is legal (but it's BETTER to get it in WRITING)!

SECRET #79: THE "HANDSHAKE" CONTRACT

I don't want to be dispensing LEGAL ADVICE, but you should know about this law before you start doing business in Canada.

If you're engaging in a relatively low-cost financial transaction (buying a used car from an individual rather than a dealer, for example), you don't need to write up a SALES contract. The person paying will typically want a RECEIPT for the money they give you as PROOF that they've paid, but you could just write on a piece of paper, "Received from _____ (their name) the sum of $_____ for the purchase of a _____ (exact make & model of the car). PAID IN FULL." Then you should BOTH SIGN it.

There are MANY websites offering free (or low-cost) TEMPLATES for legal contracts, but a LOT of business in Canada is done with a "handshake" contract. Let's say you want to finish your basement. A contractor comes and gives you a written (or verbal) estimate. You've checked at least TWO other contractors, so you know this is a reasonable price. You should pay them HALF of their price UP FRONT (to cover the cost of materials) and tell them you'll pay the remainder when the basement is finished "To MY SATISFACTION." Then you shake hands. That's a LEGAL CONTRACT here.

Secret #80:
SMALL CLAIMS COURT

If you have a legal dispute under $35,000 (in Ontario, in 2023) you can go to Small Claims Court without a lawyer to sue that person.

SECRET #80: SMALL CLAIMS COURT

A lot of the time, the handshake contract is fine, and people do what they say they'll do, when they say they'll do it.

But if they DON'T (for example, finish your basement for the price they promised, or in the timeframe they promised), you may not want to pay the 2nd half of the money you agreed upon.

Withholding the money MIGHT be enough incentive for them to deliver what they promised, but they might decide instead to take you to Small Claims Court (if the amount is under $35,000 – in Ontario, at least).

You don't have to have a lawyer in Small Claims Court, but it's a good idea. Most lawyers will meet with you for 20-30 minutes the first time for FREE. They will listen to your story, and then give you their opinion on whether you would WIN in court. If you decide to proceed, you will need to pay them a retainer (the amount varies from lawyer to lawyer).

Without a written contract, the judge will listen to each of you tell your side of the story, and then make a decision. Because he or she has no way of knowing WHO is telling the TRUTH, the outcome is usually 50/50.

Secret #81:

Men & Women do NOT Earn EQUAL PAY

Despite the LAW, women in Canada earn 87¢ for every $1.00 that a man earns.

SECRET #81: THE GENDER PAY GAP

There are complex reasons why men in Canada earn about 15% MORE than women, but often the bottom line is that women often sacrifice their careers to take care of children, and men don't.

Women often refuse higher-paying jobs because they often come with increased demands for their time. Many senior managers in Canada work 60-80 hours per week. Since they are paid a salary, the law about the maximum number of work hours per week (44 hours) doesn't apply. Many women aren't willing to accept those extended hours because it would mean less time with their kids.

The law in Canada calls for "equal pay for equal work" regardless of gender, race or other differences. In REALITY, though, how do you prove that 2 people are EXACTLY as well qualified for the job, and/or are doing EXACTLY the same job? Basically, you CAN'T, and this is one of the other reasons that women earn less than men.

Women's earnings relative to men's have improved dramatically in Canada, but we are nowhere NEAR pay equity.

Secret #82:
The POLICE are our FRIENDS

The police in Canada are well paid and well respected, and are therefore mostly friendly & helpful.

SECRET #82: THE POLICE are GOOD

Another thing I was taught in my TESL course was that around the world, police are often poorly paid and understaffed, and that this leads to corruption, where the police may be the WORST criminals.

This ISN'T true in most of Canada. Here, police officers earn about $61,000 a year. This isn't WEALTH, of course, but it's a LIVING WAGE. Coupled with the Canadian values of RESPECT & TOLERANCE, what we've ended up with are police officers who are essentially our FRIENDS.

Of course, there are incidents of racism and violence. I'm not pretending that our police are SAINTS. I just want you to know that for the most part, you can TRUST police officers (unless you are a CRIMINAL – then it's best to AVOID them).

And (as I said in **Secret #73**), you shouldn't try to BRIBE a police officer. Realistically, there might be some who would take a bribe, but for the most part, all you're doing is getting yourself into MORE trouble than you were already in.

I think of police officers as brothers, sons, uncles, and DADs – and sisters, daughters, aunts and MOMs. They have families that they care about, the same as WE do.

Secret #83:
DIVERSITY is the LAW

Canadian Laws state that you cannot be DISCRIMINATED against based on your age, gender, race, ethnicity or sexual orientation.

SECRET #83: DIVERSITY

As you'll see at the END of this book, Canada is by NO means a PARADISE. Problems that exist in other countries exist HERE, too.

One of the DIFFERENCES is that Canada's Human Rights Code provides LEGAL protection against discrimination based on your age, gender, race, religion, ethnicity, sexual orientation, etc.

Especially in our large urban centres (Vancouver, Toronto, and Montreal), your workplace or neighbourhood may very well contain more of a MIXTURE of humanity than you've EVER seen in one place.

What that means is that a large group of people, often with VERY different VALUES & ETHICS, are usually SUCCESSFUL in working or living together because they practice TOLERANCE.

However, if you experience HARASSMENT or DISCRIMINATION ANYWHERE, you can get help in challenging it. For example, contact the Ontario Human Rights Tribunal. Being denied an apartment or being harassed by someone based on your race, colour, religion or other difference, is AGAINST THE LAW (NOT just at WORK).

Keep NOTES of DATES & DETAILS, because the police are more likely to believe you the more information you provide.

Secret #84:
FAMILY VIOLENCE

It is NOT legal to hit or threaten your wife, husband, child or parent in Canada. You can go to JAIL for doing this.

Spanking your child is legal within LIMITS.

SECRET #84: DOMESTIC VIOLENCE

Sadly, many of the violent crimes that are committed in Canada are versions of domestic violence – men hitting their wives, wives hitting their husbands, parents hitting children, or adults hitting aging parents.

Luckily, this type of crime isn't common in Canada, but it DOES happen. Because WOMEN are the most common VICTIMS of domestic violence, there are MANY organizations in Canada to help women escape from abusive relationships.

Google: *"women's shelter _____" (your city).*

It's important to note that in Canada, EMOTIONAL abuse and VERBAL abuse are ALSO not acceptable. No one should threaten your safety! My ESL students look at me like I'm CRAZY when I tell them this.

They say things like, "Men YELL. It's how they ARE." I respond that in Canada, this is considered ABUSE. You don't need to be BRUISED to be HURT.

SPANKING: our law states, "Parents/caregivers can only use corrective force (or physical punishment) that is minor or 'transitory and trifling' in nature." That is, not hard enough to bruise or mark.

Secret #85:
Children – HOME ALONE?

The laws vary by province/territory, but in general, it is not acceptable to leave a child under 12 home alone. (In Ontario, it's 16.)

SECRET #85: WHAT AGE CAN KIDS STAY HOME ALONE?

In case you don't get the reference, it's a movie about a family who accidentally leaves their 8-year-old son "home alone" while they go on a Christmas vacation. It's a funny movie, but in REALITY, you CAN'T leave a child alone at home in Canada if they are under 12 (16 in Ontario).

The legality of "Latchkey Kids" (kids who get home 1-2 hours before their parents do and may stay home alone until the parents return from work) is a kind of legal 'grey area' in Canada. However, if your child ends up hurt or scared by being home alone and the police get involved, Child Welfare Services may ALSO become involved, and parents can end up being charged with child neglect or abuse.

Actually, any person under the age of 18 (when we become a Legal Adult) is defined as a CHILD by our Child Protection laws, so even leaving your 17-year-old home alone while you go on vacation might get you into trouble.

It's BEST to make sure your child is supervised by an ADULT when you are not at home.

Secret #86:

How LONG do You Have to STAY in SCHOOL?

Legally, you have to stay in school until you are 18. In reality, if you leave school at 16 or 17, neither the child nor the parents will be charged.

SECRET #86: DROPPING OUT OF SCHOOL

Canadians place a strong value on education. In fact, if you Google: ***2014 Education at a Glance report by the OECD***, you'll see that Canada has the highest percentage (53%) among member countries of adults aged 25-64 who have obtained some form of post-secondary education – that is, education beyond high school.

That said, about a 16% of high school students in Canada drop out before they complete high school. This is a serious problem because there is a STRONG correlation between lack of a high school diploma and unemployment.

The LAW is that you MUST stay in school until you are 18, but in REALITY, the police won't prosecute a 16 or 17 year old, or their parents, if that child stops attending school. Under the age of 16, any child who does not attend school is considered "truant" and the police can show up on your doorstep to ESCORT your child to school.

If you don't force your under-16 child to go to school, this can be deemed CHILD NEGLECT, and you can be ARRESTED and CHARGED.

Bottom line? – STAY in SCHOOL!

Secret #87:

When are you a LEGAL ADULT?

You are considered a legal adult at 18 years old. You can get married, vote, buy property, etc. The DRINKING AGE varies by province/territory. In Ontario, it's 19.

SECRET #87: WHEN ARE YOU A LEGAL ADULT?

You are a legal adult at 18 years old in Canada. At this age, parents are no longer financially responsible for the child (though individual Child Support agreements might affect this). Parents in Canada often continue to provide financial support to their adult children while they go to university or until they find a full-time job, but the law doesn't require this.

The legal age to leave home (live independent of your parents) varies between provinces and territories, but is usually 16 to 18 years old. In Ontario, for example, you COULD leave home at 16, but if you leave and there is NO evidence of ABUSE, your parents are not obligated to pay your living expenses.

The 'drinking age' – the age where you are legally entitled to buy and consume alcohol – again varies, but is at LEAST 18 (19 in Ontario).

At 18, you have the right to VOTE and are considered an adult in the criminal justice system.

You can start working at age 12 with your parents' consent, and at age 15 without parental consent. You can get married at 16 with parental consent, and 18 without it.

Google: *AGE of MAJORITY in Canada* for more details.

Secret #88:

Permanent Residents Have (Almost) the SAME RIGHTS as Citizens

The main differences are that a Permanent Resident CAN'T VOTE or get a CANADIAN PASSPORT.

SECRET #88: PERMANENT RESIDENTS (PR)

If you have Permanent Resident status in Canada, you are entitled to almost ALL of the same rights and freedoms as a Canadian citizen.

You have a right to free healthcare; to work, study and live wherever you want; and you are protected by our Charter of Rights and Freedoms. You CAN'T vote or get a Canadian Passport until you become a CITIZEN.

Many of my PR students are NERVOUS about their ability to stay in Canada, but you can live your WHOLE LIFE here without becoming a citizen. The only REAL requirement to maintain your PR status is a 'residency' requirement – you have to have stayed in Canada for at least 730 days during the last five years.

SCAMS: WARNING! Revenue Canada or Immigration Canada will NEVER phone you to demand money. If you get a call like this, it's a SCAM. DON'T PAY.

Many PRs travel back and forth to their home countries for business or personal reasons, and as long as you meet the residency requirement, there's no problem. You can lose your PR status in only a few situations – if you are convicted of a serious crime, for example, or are found to have received your status through fraud.

Secret #89:
PETS ARE FAMILY

In Canada, we treat our pets like PEOPLE. If you hurt an animal deliberately, you can go to JAIL.

SECRET #89: PETS ARE FAMILY!

One of the BIGGEST Culture Shocks that I hear about from my immigrant students is how Canadians feel about their PETS. A dog or a cat in our home is 'he' or 'she', NOT 'it'. That's because for MOST Canadians, their pet is a TREASURED part of their FAMILY.

When we make small talk and ask each other about our spouses and kids, we may also ask about PETS, especially if they're very young (puppies or kittens). Some people bring their pet with them to get-togethers, and I have seen one or two at WEDDINGS!

One of the BEST ways to make friends with your new neighbours is to get a PUPPY and start taking it for walks around the neighbourhood. People who never said a WORD to you will suddenly come over and ask you about your dog!

If you don't like pets, it's best NOT to SAY so. While we respect other people's right to their opinions, 'pet lovers' may be PREJUDICED against 'pet haters'.

If you are caught deliberately injuring an animal, you can go to JAIL. If you are guilty of ABUSE or NEGLECT of an animal, you can go to JAIL. We have strict laws protecting farm animals, too.

Secret #90:
WE'RE NOT VERY RELIGIOUS

Only about 15% of Canadians attend church on a weekly basis, despite the fact that MOST Canadians say they believe in God.

SECRET #90: "SPIRITUAL BUT NOT RELIGIOUS"

While about 80% of Canadians believe in 'God' or a 'higher power', about only 15% attend places of worship weekly.

There has been a steady decline in church attendance for the past 50 years in Canada. When I've asked the people around me why they think this is, most of them have told me that they believe in SCIENCE, not RELIGION.

Nevertheless, Canadian culture and LAWS are STRONGLY influenced by Christian values (respect, honesty, fidelity and trustworthiness, among others). Of course, these values are present in MOST world religions, but they came to Canada with Christianity.

Our CHARTER OF RIGHTS AND FREEDOMS guarantees freedom of religion, so it is illegal to discriminate against you because of your religion. That DOESN'T mean it doesn't happen, though.

In June 2019, Quebec passed a controversial 'Secularism' bill. Google: *Quebec Bill 21*

Bill 21 formally BANS 'public officials' in Quebec – teachers, police officers, judges and many others – from wearing religion-related items – such as hijabs, turbans, kippas, and crucifixes – in the course of their duties.

Secret #91:
Complain POLITELY

Of course you'll have problems here, too! But when you complain, DON'T YELL. Be POLITE but INSISTENT and you will usually get what you want.

SECRET #91: COMPLAINING EFFECTIVELY

I don't know how people complain in other cultures, but in Canada, we complain POLITELY! We don't YELL. In fact, the more you yell, the LESS successful you are to be with your complaint!! Oh! And it doesn't hurt to SMILE (believe it or not)!

Most people, even people born here, don't seem to understand how IMPORTANT it is to TELL the person EXACTLY WHAT YOU WANT. Effective complaining should make it EASY for the person to satisfy you. If you're upset, but you don't make it CLEAR what you want, all you're doing is ATTACKING the other person! Say something like, "I would like a full refund on this defective _____ (name of machine)" rather than saying, "This _____ is a piece of GARBAGE!"

The best way to complain is to be POLITE but INSISTENT. If you complain, and the other person doesn't take the actions you have asked for, don't show anger. Just keep repeating your request in a QUIET, POLITE voice.

Complaining in an email can also be very effective, particularly if you're polite and tell the person EXACTLY what they can do to make you happy.

Keep in mind – Canadians HATE conflict! They'd usually rather do ANYTHING to make you happy rather than ARGUE with you!

Secret #92:
Use the "Bad News Sandwich"

When we deliver bad news, we usually "sandwich" it in between positive statements. BEGIN & END by saying something NICE!

SECRET #92: THE "BAD NEWS SANDWICH"

You might have already been on the RECEIVING end of this technique without realizing it! My immigrant students tell me this can be VERY CONFUSING at work.

For example, if you're in sales, your boss might say something like, "We're REALLY happy to have you on our team. (GOOD news) Unfortunately, your last quarter results didn't meet our expectations. (BAD news) Why don't you ask _____ to help you improve your sales pitch?" (POSITIVE suggestion)

Is your boss HAPPY with you, or MAD at you??? Actually, **MAD**. The same goes for the comments on your children's REPORT CARDS. The teacher might write, "_____ is doing better in class. He/She is making progress in working with partners for group projects. Good work!" You might MISTAKE "making progress" for GOOD news, but it really ISN'T. (It means he/she was TERRIBLE but is a bit better now!) (see **Secret #56**)

How to understand a "bad news sandwich"?
Only the MIDDLE part of the statement is IMPORTANT.

Secret #93:

Why we PRETEND we are EQUALS

"EQUALITY" is a central value to Canadians. So we address our boss by their first name & we don't talk about money so we can PRETEND we are equal.

SECRET #93: WHY WE PRETEND TO BE EQUALS

Many of my immigrant students find it WEIRD that Canadians REFUSE to talk about MONEY. Of course, people are INTERESTED in how much we PAID for our new shoes, or new car, or house; and how much we EARN. But we can't ASK.

The REASON for this is that as long as we don't talk about money, we can PRETEND to be equals. But if I paid $38 for MY new shoes, and you paid $700 for yours in Italy, 'equality' flies out the window!

EQUALITY is a CENTRAL VALUE in Canadian culture. It's part of our Charter of Rights and Freedoms, and it's one of the reasons that many of our ancestors came to Canada in the first place – to rise above the social class they were born in. "EQUAL OPPORTUNITY" is probably why MANY of you came here! Of course, there is NO such thing, but I believe BETTER opportunities ARE possible here.

PRETEND EQUALITY is also the reason that I call everyone in my company by their first names. The use of FIRST NAMES ONLY in Canada is another Culture Shock for many immigrants, but it's part of our attempt to treat each other as equals.

It's important to remember that I am NOT equal to my boss and must show respect and do whatever he or she tells me to do (see **Secret #71**).

Secret #94:
The BAD News:
Racism

Yes, there IS racism here. Canadians don't talk about it much because we HIDE it by sounding SUPER-FRIENDLY while denying you a Job or Housing.

SECRET #94: THE BAD NEWS: RACISM

Many people come to Canada to ESCAPE RACISM. Unfortunately, it exists HERE, too – and it seems to be INCREASING rather than decreasing. Our Federal Government allocated $45 million toward an anti-racism strategy from 2019-2022, so it's not like the country doesn't KNOW there's a problem.

I've travelled extensively in the United States, and it seems to me that the biggest DIFFERENCE is that in many places there, racism is OVERT.

In Canada, POLITENESS can be a MASK that covers prejudice and xenophobia (fear of foreigners). Racism is also a SHAMEFUL SECRET. If your family has racist beliefs, most people know that they aren't something you can TALK ABOUT in PUBLIC.

Our Charter of Rights and Freedoms is supposed to PROTECT you from DISCRIMINATION based on race. The TROUBLE is, how do you PROVE that the reason you didn't get the job, or were refused an apartment, was because of your race?

Hopefully, Canada will address these issues BETTER in the future.

Secret #95:
The BAD News:
Sexism

Women DON'T have the same opportunities for employment or advancement that men have. WORSE, we DON'T get the same quality of HEALTHCARE.

SECRET #95: THE BAD NEWS: SEXISM

Many women around the world STRUGGLE with achieving BASIC HUMAN RIGHTS, let alone EQUALITY. And I WISH I could tell you that Canada offers EQUAL OPPORTUNITIES for men and women. But it just isn't TRUE.

Not only do women earn LESS than men (see **Secret #81**), but we also don't get HIRED or PROMOTED into MANAGEMENT as often as men do. This IS changing. Opportunities for women are MUCH better NOW than they were 50 years ago. But we still have a long way to go.

My OTHER – perhaps more SERIOUS concern about sexism in Canada – is that women simply AREN'T taken as SERIOUSLY by our medical professionals. Canada's Heart and Stroke Association says that 78% of women's early warning signs of heart attack are DISMISSED by medical professionals, and that women who go to the hospital with a possible heart attack are MORE LIKELY to DIE than men.

And that's EVEN THOUGH nearly 50% of all family physicians in Canada are WOMEN. It's a SYSTEMIC problem where medical schools (perhaps subconsciously) train doctors NOT to take women as seriously as men.

Secret #96:
The BAD News:
Ageism

Older people DON'T automatically get RESPECT here, and older workers have a harder time finding a job, too. DYE your grey hair!

SECRET #96: THE BAD NEWS: AGEISM

Unfortunately, unlike many other countries, being OLDER in Canada does NOT mean that you get treated with RESPECT. In fact, often the OPPOSITE is true. Older people may receive worse Customer Service than younger people.

Worse than that, even though workers aged 55+ make up nearly 40% of Canada's workforce, it can be MORE DIFFICULT for an older worker to find a job in Canada. Employers fear that older workers "won't stay" very long – that training them isn't a "good investment".

It's ILLEGAL for an interviewer to ask you your age, but he/she might ask you, "Do you have any plans for retirement?" You might also hear statements like, "We think you're over-qualified for this position," You have too much experience," or "You might get bored." These may all simply be euphemisms for, "You're TOO OLD."

Like other forms of prejudice here, it's hard to PROVE that the reason you didn't get the job was your AGE. That's why I recommend that if you're applying for work here and you have grey hair, DYE IT.

Secret #97:
The BAD News:
Social CLASSES

YES, we have them here, too:
the upper class,
the middle class,
the working class,
the working poor
& the poor.

SECRET #97: THE BAD NEWS: SOCIAL CLASSES

I find it INTERESTING that my immigrant students think that we don't have social classes in Canada. In fact, many people BORN here would ALSO argue that we don't have social classes. But the REALITY is that, just like everywhere else, there are groups of people with MORE MONEY than the rest of us, and groups of people who automatically get MORE RESPECT than the rest of us.

Like everything else in this book, I'm OVER-SIMPLIFYING this. (You could write a book on any ONE of these secrets!) One of the IMPORTANT things to understand, at least, is that MONEY does NOT necessarily equate to HIGHER STATUS in Canadian society.

For example, an experienced PLUMBER earns approximately the SAME as a full-time UNIVERSITY PROFESSOR in Canada (approximately $100,000 per year), but the professor gets FAR more respect!

Celebrities or professional athletes are some of our richest citizens, but most Canadians value nurses, doctors, scientists, farmers and veterinarians more highly; and politicians are the LEAST respected, right BELOW car salespeople!

The reason this matters is that if you are perceived as "lower class", you may not receive the same quality of healthcare as someone who is perceived as "middle" or "upper" class. You are also more likely to be arrested (and convicted). *That's why, when I have an appointment with a doctor, dentist or government official, I wear business clothes and do my hair and makeup as if I was going for a job interview.*

Secret #98:

The BAD News:

Our SHAMEFUL treatment of Indigenous Peoples

Canada has a sad history with regard to our treatment of indigenous peoples.

SECRET #98: THE BAD NEWS: How we treat our INDIGENOUS PEOPLES

One time that *I* experienced Culture Shock was when Nelson Mandela was released from prison in South Africa, and my class was talking about apartheid. I was deploring this systematic segregation based on race, when one of my students said, "Well, you have apartheid in Canada, too." I was OUTRAGED. We do NOT! "Oh, yeah? How about the way you treat your indigenous peoples?" OUCH.

Canada has 3 groups of indigenous peoples: First Nations (what we used to call "Indians" – no longer a polite term), Inuit and Métis. We have a shameful history regarding our treatment of indigenous peoples, from stealing their land to kidnapping their children and putting them in "Residential Schools" where the teachers attempted to convert them to Christianity, often ABUSED (and sometimes KILLED) them. September 30th is "Orange Shirt Day" in Canada: a day to remember the indigenous children who died in residential schools in Canada.

Today, there is still a lot of prejudice against our indigenous peoples, but no one will talk about it. Our government is trying to apologize and make amends for some of the systemic racism against indigenous peoples in Canada, but we still have a long way to go.

Secret #99:

The BAD News:

French vs. English Canadians

There is also prejudice (BOTH ways!) between French-speakers & English-speakers.

SECRET #99: THE BAD NEWS: FRENCH vs. ENGLISH

Another form of discrimination that exists in Canada is between French-speaking and English-speaking Canadians. If you know anything about the history of France and England, you might be surprised that the nation of Canada was formed principally by these historic ENEMIES.

Canada was originally colonized in the 1600s by the French, and it wasn't until the 1763 "Treaty of Paris" that Canada was officially taken over by the British. My mother is French-Canadian, and she told me that the French were "second-class citizens" in Canada. In fact, until the **Official Languages Act** in 1969, many French speakers were not able to access government services or even health care in their own language!

Quebec today has language laws that may exclude English speakers in much the same way. Street and highway signs in Quebec are French-only. Legal contracts and documents at work MUST be in French (even if the company is English-speaking).

When visiting Quebec, if you speak even a little French, you will be more welcomed. Say, "Bonjour" for "Hello", "S'il vous plaît" for "Please", "Merci" for "Thank you" and "Au revoir" for "Goodbye".

Secret #100:
S.A.D.

(Seasonal Affective Disorder)

Our winters can be LONG & DARK. You need to TAKE STEPS to cope with S.A.D.

SECRET #100: Seasonal Affective Disorder (S.A.D.)

In wintertime in Canada, the days get shorter and the light gets weaker (It's not your IMAGINATION!) Many Canadian (including ME) suffer emotionally and often physically in the winter. Our immune system can also get depressed by the low light. The symptoms can include:

- Oversleeping
- Craving for foods high in carbohydrates
- Weight gain
- Tiredness or low energy

The GOOD NEWS is, you CAN learn to cope with S.A.D. There are 4 steps that I recommend:

1. Spend at LEAST 20-30 minutes OUTDOORS each day (sunny or not). Ultraviolet light (UV) has been shown to have a positive effect on our moods. My mother always says: "There's NO such thing as bad weather; only people who aren't DRESSED PROPERLY for it!"

2. Take Vitamin D (Doctors recommend adults take 1200 IU per day. Be careful not to take more than this, and children under the age of 3 should only take it under a doctor's guidance.)

3. Use a "full spectrum" or "daylight" light bulb (NOT fluorescent!) near where you or your children usually study or sit.

4. SOCIALIZE! Everyone knows that spending time with family & friends lifts our mood. If you can socialize outdoors, *BONUS!*

Secret #101:
The GOOD News:

Canada is still a land of opportunity. If you work hard and adapt to Canadian culture, you can have a VERY HAPPY life here!

WELCOME!!

#101: CANADA IS a land of OPPORTUNITY

Now that I've scared and/or DESPRESSED you, I want to END by saying that I LOVE Canada; that I believe the Canada still IS a "land of opportunity" and that you CAN have a WONDERFUL life here!

If there is ONE SECRET that will go a LONG WAY toward your SUCCESS in Canada, it is **Secret #3** – SMILE!

A POSTIVE ATTITUDE will really help you succeed in Canada. We are, for the most part, OPTIMISTS who see good things in the future, and if you can EMBRACE this attitude, you will make friends and succeed at work.

My grandparents, who first came to Canada, had a HARD life. My parents had a BETTER life than my grandparents. I have had a BETTER life than my parents, and my kids are having BETTER lives than I have had.

THIS is why you come to Canada. WELCOME!

BEST WISHES for SUCCESS and a LONG, HAPPY LIFE in Canada!

Kate Maven

WHERE TO LEARN MORE ABOUT CANADA:

Here are some ways to learn more about Canadian Culture:

BOOK: "Always My Child: A Parent's Guide to Understanding Your Gay, Lesbian, Bisexual, Transgendered, or Questioning Son or Daughter"

GOOGLE:

- settlement.org ★ (LOTS of GREAT info!)
- meetup.com (put in your Postal Code)
- Telehealth Ontario
- Canada Child Support Calculator
- Finding a job – Canada.ca
- What is Enhanced Language Training
- Toastmasters
- Starting a business - Canada.ca
- Raptor's Super Fan
- Child Welfare Services (+ your city/town)
- social register in communications in Canada
- Age of Majority in Canada
- Canadian Human Rights Code
- Women's shelter _____ (your city/town)
- wix.com (free websites)
- vistaprint.ca (low-cost business cards)

11843767R00118